Open Season

An Angler's Life In New Zealand

Open
Season

DAVE WITHEROW

RANDOM HOUSE
NEW ZEALAND

A RANDOM HOUSE BOOK published by Random House New Zealand
18 Poland Road, Glenfield, Auckland, New Zealand

For more information about our titles go to www.randomhouse.co.nz

A catalogue record for this book is available from the National Library
of New Zealand

Random House New Zealand is part of the Random House Group
New York   London   Sydney   Auckland   Delhi   Johannesburg

First published 2014

© 2014 text and images Dave Witherow; image page 153 courtesy
Dougal Rillstone; image page 227 courtesy Ray Keown

The moral rights of the author have been asserted

ISBN 978 1 77553 715 1
eISBN 978 1 77553 716 8

Design: Carla Sy
Cover photograph: photonewzealand/Darryl Torckler
Fly illustration: shutterstock/Epsen E
Map by Geographx Ltd

Printed in New Zealand by Printlink

This publication is printed on paper pulp sourced from sustainably
grown and managed forests, using Elemental Chlorine Free (ECF)
bleaching, and printed with 100% vegetable-based inks.

This title is also available as an eBook

For Brian Turner

Contents

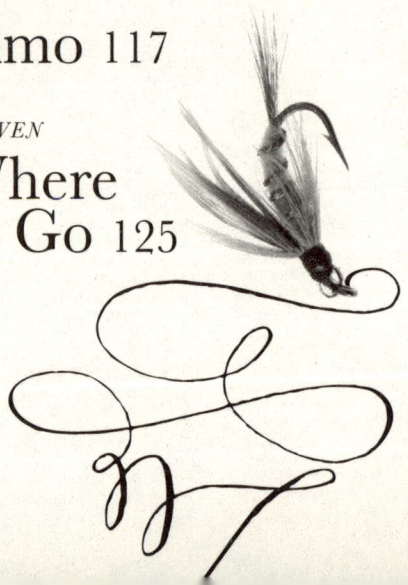

Foreword

The best fishing is a larger-than-life experience. It lifts us out of our normal existences and places us in wild environments where every moment is informed by a heightened sense of alertness, energy and secret understanding. And the best books about fishing convey this experience and remind us of its magical intensity.

Dave Witherow's account of some of his glorious, perilous, frustrating and hilarious days on some of the world's great rivers is one of the finest in the genre. It is full of insight, sound sense, good humour, modesty, exaggeration, subtle information and adventure — but beyond all these attributes it enters into a territory of incidents and encounters where we are reminded of moments of awareness that have had an almost mystical impact on our own lives and outlooks.

The first time I met Dave he stopped for a few seconds to say hullo then he looked past me and said, 'There has to be a fish in the eye of that ripple.' He slipped down a bank quickly, made one short cast and landed a pretty, three-pound brownie.

It was an impressive display of skill, but if he thought he could get away with pulling a neat trick like that on first meeting an incompetent like myself he has been made to pay for it ever since, as I have consistently held him back to help me out of deep water, then I have often enough followed up these performances by managing to fluke a fish where it should never have been and causing him pain by breaking all the rules of orthodoxy.

Flying into remote territories with Dave, in one of his beautiful little aeroplanes, then landing on a stretch of river gravel or skimming inches over a barbed-wire fence into an unlikely paddock, has often made me aware that for decades he has been trying to scare off most of the characters in this book and leave him in perfect peace. But the fact of the matter is that we refuse to be intimidated, for we have come to realise that we have been appointed to haunt his life with all the dark and inexorable force of a ghastly destiny.

I have frequently asked myself how it is possible for all the fine people who have discovered themselves described and frequently derided in Dave's regular column in *Fish & Game* to stick around year after year and put up with it all, and there are two simple answers.

The first is that we no longer sleep out in pup tents. We now have beds to lie in, hot showers, an electric stove, a log fire summer and winter, and excellent wines to sip in easy chairs. These comforts have softened and stretched our powers of toleration and endurance.

But the second answer is even more important. The sheer pleasure of Dave's abilities and craftsmanship always save the day. His writing has the same relaxed, discursive and illuminating brilliance of his conversation. There are no limits to its horizons.

Kevin Ireland
August 2014

The Dingleburn.

The Size of Trout

Trout, since the earliest days of fishing for sport, have been weighed in pounds and ounces, and measured in feet and inches.

There are centuries of tradition in this, and poetry as well, and whatever the convenience of the metric system, it has no place in the evocative language of angling. We catch five-pounders, if we are lucky — not two-point-two-seven-kilogrammers. That is the way it has always been, and I hope will always remain.

And for the same reasons, in the pages that follow, our heroes march and climb and explore the terrain in time-honoured miles, and never in kilometres.

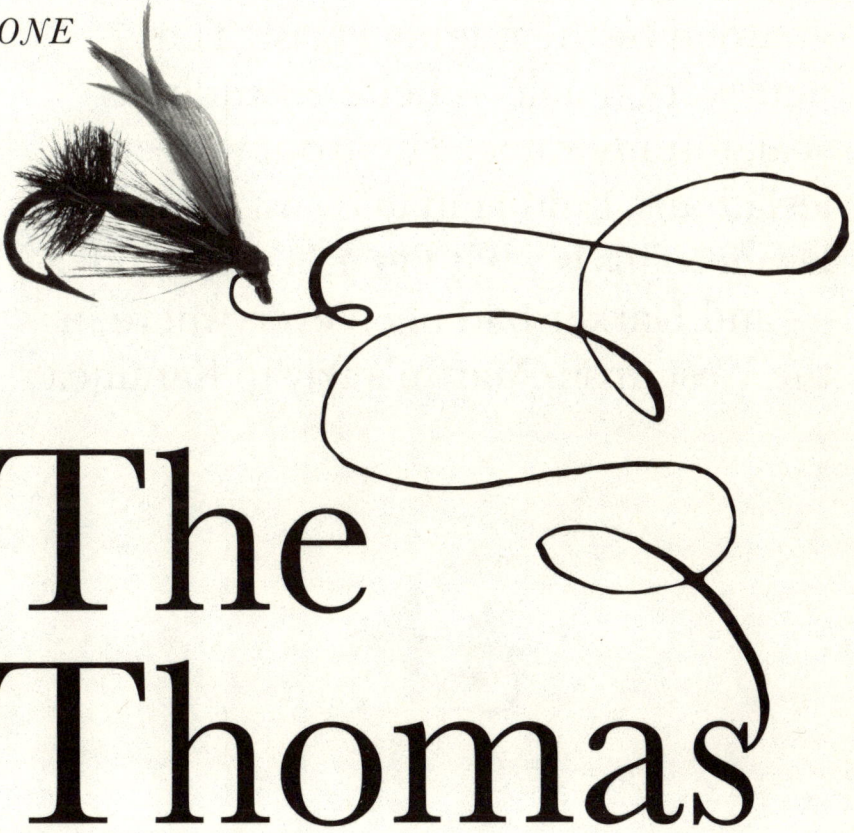

ONE

The Thomas

For years I dreamed of the Thomas. It was a faraway, unvisited paradise, guarded by the mighty Haast. The deer were docile as heifers, tender as veal, innumerable. The trout were all leviathans, unimaginable east of the Divide. This is what Peter Harker said — and Harker had been everywhere in the West, from Martin's Bay to Karamea.

Harker was a hunter, and an explorer of the Coast's last hidden places. He was an angler of the old-fashioned school, a specialist, an exponent of the nickel spinner — which he favoured as an all-round lure when roast venison grew monotonous and the diet needed a lift. Four-pound trout were ideal, he thought, not too big — a decent pair of fillets and nothing gone to waste. The Thomas was a pain in the arse in that regard: too many bloody ten-pounders.

I organised several missions, spanning several seasons, but there were too many good rivers on the way, and we never got near the Thomas. On the first effort, after weeks of planning, we stopped for a beer in Wanaka, where Two-Pies heard a rumour that a green beetle hatch in the Hunter had addled the rainbows' brains. There was no talking the boys out of that one, and off we raced to the head of the lake, only to find a dust-storm in progress, the river filthy, and the beetles lying low.

The following year I tried again. Dougal had a bug, and there were just three of us this time — Turner, myself, and Two-Pies. We got past Wanaka safely enough, and made it as far as the Makarora, only to be diverted by the lure of the Young, where, for once, the rumours were well founded. There were swags of big trout, and no other anglers. We had the river to ourselves for five glorious days. And so it went: too many competing attractions, and a crew too easily diverted. The Thomas seemed unattainable.

In the early autumn of 1978 we made another attempt. There was heavy weather in Southland, and Turner wanted to call it off, but I persuaded him the forecast was good, and anyway there hadn't been that much rain in the mountains. Dougal and Two-Pies were keen, but they both had to work that Friday, so it was nearly dark when we finally got on the road.

Two-Pies drove. It was his car: a new Datsun, packed solid, with a pallet of gear on the roof. We stopped for a leak at Roxburgh, where I manufactured a fat cigar and dug a bottle of wine out of the cases Two-Pies had stored in the boot; it was going to be a long trip and we might as well relax. When we got back in the car I lit the thing and passed it around — but the others were being responsible.

The road climbs steeply above Roxburgh, away from the dam and into the naked mountains. The Datsun was warm and comfortable, filled with aromatic smoke. We had a heater and a tape deck, and the road ahead would surely, this time, lead us to the river of dreams. Turner, sitting in the front, accepted a swig of wine. A rare, illicit smile illuminated his face. He shuffled through the tapes and selected one and put it in the machine. And the car leapt forward, at Two-Pies' urging, to the rhythm of Fleetwood Mac.

We had agreed to bypass Wanaka, and the next siphon stop was on the big headland beyond Hawea, looking across to the mouth of the Dingleburn and westward into the Alps. It was surprisingly chilly outside as we lined up in the moonlight with the vast surface of the lake below us gleaming into the distance. Mountain air washed through our lungs, scented with thyme, and the distant peaks above the Hunter glowed red from the vanished sun. Then we were back in the car and warm again, cruising through the Neck between the lakes and along the high, winding shoreline and into the Makarora valley.

Maybe, suggested Dougal, we should stop at the campground — put up the tent, or possibly get a cabin. It was going to be cold, and we'd be better starting off in the morning well fed and rested and raring to go. It would be comfortable in the campground. We could light a fire and have a feed. I agreed, and so did Turner, but there was no persuading Two-Pies, who was still behind the wheel. We were on the road, he said, and we'd stay on the road — and anyway it was midnight and the bloody campground would be shut. We had left town to get away from people and civilisation in general, and that included campgrounds. He sank the boot. Warren Zevon was on: Werewolves of London, full bore. Goodbye Makarora.

I assumed from this performance that there would be no stopping till we reached the Thomas. But at Cameron Creek Two-Pies suddenly stood on the brakes and swerved off the road and up a steep bank towards some trees. This is it, you bastards, he said, home for the night. Get out.

The silvered earth was crunchy, and beside the creek a swathe of ice-rimed tussock glittered in the moonlight. Turner stumbled around and located a bench of near-level ground he said would do. It was studded with boulders and corrugated with the roots of beech trees, but there didn't seem to be anywhere better. Not that I cared anyway, for I had a fat air bed and even a pump to blow it up with. I also had a new sleeping bag, recommended by Ed Hillary himself — an identical bag, or so the advertisement had said, to the one Ed had used in the Himalayas. This should be a fair workout, I thought: rocks, roots, and a gulag frost. Two-Pies blew up his fancy bed as well, but Turner and Dougal, masochists both, laid out their threadbare bags on the hostile earth and climbed in, fully clad.

Ed was right. The Everest was a thermal wonder, and I slept till the first vigilante sandflies got moving in the morning. Turner was already busy, cooking breakfast on the Coleman, and Dougal seemed to have disappeared. I got up, and so did Two-Pies. We had billy tea, the big tin mugs hot in our clasped hands. Then bacon, beans, honey and toast. The Makarora was coming to life, thin trails of vapour drifting up from the bush, limning the gully ridgelines. A robin arrived and was fed, and then Dougal showed up, puffing hard. He had been running since dawn, up and down the gravel road, and now he was back to normal. The sky was clear, the palest blue — just a wisp of cloud at the head of the valley. We were in business. We simply couldn't go wrong.

The Haast Pass, approached from the east, is deceptive. Towards the summit there is an easy gradient through stunted beech, and the great Divide of the Southern Alps is flat and barely perceptible. On the western side the trees are few and scattered, and the road drops down through sparse cover and open vistas into the headwaters of the nascent river. This is a spacious country, exposed to the sky, the road swinging in level curves past yellow meadows of tussock grass bordering a sparkling stream.

Soon, however, the valley tightens. The granite shoulders of the hills close in and the last river flat gives way to a slit-like ravine. The road angles ever more steeply, narrowing into a winding ledge dynamited out of the mountainside. On the left, pressing close, is a wall of black rock. Water spatters on the windscreen, dripping from a rough-hewn ceiling hung with moss and fern that obliterates most of the sky.

Far below the road, in the depths of the gorge, the river has been swallowed in the deep-piled wreckage of avalanche and earthquake. Slabs of granite, the size of tanks, lie skewed atop each other, their fractured surfaces gleaming here and there in eruptions of pent-up water. Mist eddies and flows, softening the raw geology, and the stripped remnants of long-dead trees jab like matchsticks from the debris. A few survivors cling forlornly, bent limbs askew, awaiting the next shrug of the mountain. There is a chill in the gorge, even at midday.

The Datsun's brakes, pushed to the limit, were puffing smoke and barely holding. Two-Pies sat braced behind the wheel, arms straight, eyes fixed, as the car slid sideways across the road and ploughed into a shoulder of piled-up rubble. It dug a deep furrow and came clear again, still going sideways, and headed for the stormwater ditch on the other side of the road. Two-Pies pumped the fading brakes, steering energetically to no effect. We hit a ridge of gravel and the car slewed almost broadside. There was a blind bend ahead, and then a short, very steep descent that ended in the twin concrete abutments of the one-way Gates of Haast. Turner leaned close: If there's a tourist parked on the bridge, he said, we're fucked.

There were no tourists, and Two-Pies kept the car on the road, rattling across the old hardwood planking and stopping on the other side. We got out and stretched extravagantly, pleased with ourselves, and walked back to the middle of the grey steel structure, and threw pebbles into the chasm. The air was cold and moist in our lungs, and the cliffs pressed close and the mountains and sky and the dark maw of the gorge were swathed alike in low-hanging cloud. There was no leavening of light. Grey clouds and grey mist, and, beneath our feet, the boom of the unseen river. A pinpoint of motion appeared, far out from the bridge, and flew towards us, sparkling. It was a dragonfly, its wings a tinsel flicker on the neon pencil of its body. It whirred past between the metal beams, close enough to touch, and dissolved in the watery air.

We drove on. The road dropped down a last steep incline and into the first mossy trees of the West Coast bush. The Haast valley opened out and there were blue windows in the sky and fresh seal on the road, and the river, released from the mountain's grip, flowed swift and clear by the big bridge at Pleasant Flat. Two-Pies pulled up in the middle of the bridge and we got out and examined the riverbed. There would have to be trout, and Dougal soon found one, a grey, shifting shadow among the big, rounded boulders. It vanished in a puff of silt — a sign from the Gods, for sure.

Beyond Pleasant Flat the country is vast and uninhabited, with high mountains on every horizon. Rainforest covers the valley floor, and the river itself is often far out of sight, and the road — a two-lane ribbon of smooth black tarmac through forest and scree — is the ultimate hoon's delight. Two-Pies, cocky again, turned up the music and opened the taps. There are so many paths, sang the Little River Band, as we powered through snaky bends down corridors of light in the harlequin evergreen jungle.

The main tributary of the Haast is the Landsborough, which comes in from the north about nine miles above the Thomas confluence. A glacier-fed, fearsome river, the Landsborough in flood dwarfs the Haast itself, and today, even from a distance, the combined rivers were impressive. Finding a ford might not be all that easy. That Haast is a dangerous bastard, said Turner. We are probably going to get wet.

The Haast Bluff was unmistakable. We parked on the road-edge, looking down on an expanse of dry shingle that had been underwater not long before. At the foot of the bluff was a long, deep pool, full of filmy green weed, but the river itself had shifted, and was now lost somewhere in a wilderness of tangled scrub that carpeted the valley floor. Turner pointed to a gap in the green wall of the opposite mountains — the entrance to the Thomas valley. He scratched his beard and grinned as if it were obligatory. Don't get too excited, he said: we'll need to have a look around.

He nominated Dougal and they got into their boots and climbed down the bluff and disappeared into the scrub, while Two-Pies and I looked for somewhere to hide the car. We found a place on a dry bench by a little creek, and then started off through tall, close-grown manuka in what we hoped was the right direction. We got to the river eventually. It was big alright, and opaque with silt. The bottom was invisible below boot depth and there were white-topped corrugations out in the middle — not a good sign, according to Two-Pies.

It was almost midday, an indigo sky. There was hardly a breath in the warming air, but the water, when we tried it, stung like early snowmelt. It was moving fast as well, and within yards of the bank we were struggling to stand in a thigh-deep, icy current. There was no chance of fording this monster — and there was no sign of Turner and Dougal.

Two-Pies was disconsolate. He stood at the edge of the river, gazing across its sweeping expanse at the unreachable opposite shore. Well, that's it, he said. We're buggered. Let's find those pricks and get out of here. He shrugged unhappily and took off upstream, barrelling through the lupins.

In the river bank, half-buried, was a five-bar wooden gate. It had drifted down from God-knows-where, a rare artefact in this wild terrain of shingle and bush and dry, intersecting channels. Two-Pies examined the gate. He fingered the wood of the exposed top rail. Larch, he said. Very nice gate — I have one in the garden at home. He hunkered down and started shovelling at the silt with his bare hands, tossing dirt between his knees like a rabbit, and hauling on the timbers of the gate. He looked up at me. Help me, you dumb bastard, he said. Dig. It floated to here, didn't it? Well, maybe it can float a bit further.

The gate was free and washed clean by the time Dougal and Turner showed up. It rocked nicely in the shallows with a couple of inches of freeboard, and Two-Pies, proprietorial, summarised the situation. No problem at all, he concluded — all we have to do is fetch the gear. It ought to be a total piece of piss. But Turner was less than impressed.

You are nuts, he said. Four packs, fishing rods and a rifle? What do you think will happen when you load them on to this? He placed one foot on the corner of the gate and pushed it under. Turner knows about boats. Turner has been wrecked, been rescued. He is an expert, his verdict final. Instantly it was gloom again — until Dougal remembered the air beds.

The raft rode high and stable once we got it assembled. The packs were on top of the gate and the gate on top of the air beds. The rifle and rods were wedged in the middle, and everything — including an underwater cross-bracing of manuka poles — was lashed together with rope. We took some photos — just in case — and then, with the raft in front of us, started into the river.

The plan was to wade as far as we could, and, when footing was lost, swim with the raft in front. The first bit went well enough, but once we hit deep water the river took over. Our most strenuous thrashing had no effect at all, and soon we were zipping along in a choppy sea of whitecaps. The cold was numbing, and, with the bulk of the packs in front of us, it was hard to see where we were going. The raft tossed about, the ropes biting into our fingers; it rode up on a great hump of fizzing water, and spun around, allowing a quick glimpse of the far shore, still distant. Things seemed slightly out of control, I thought, but Turner kept firing out orders. The rest of the crew kept kicking.

The buffeting died down after a while and the waves got smaller and then there was a beach directly in front, and Two-Pies, the tallest, reported he could feel the bottom. We scrabbled for grip and, half-swimming, half-shoving, grounded the raft on a shelf of gravel.

We were on dry land, but not, as we soon discovered, on the other side of the river. We were on a sand bar — a gravel island covered with lupins, invisible from where we had started. Ahead lay another channel, narrower than the one we had just survived, but faster and seamed with rapids. There was a high, bare cliff on the opposite shore, tree-crested, and from the swift, deep water that swept its base stood a graveyard of fresh-fallen timber. We were trapped. There was no open water. There was no possibility of getting through this barrage intact, and further downstream was no more encouraging — the white rip of the Thomas inflow, and then rock walls for miles.

But it was noon, and the air was warm. The pea gravel of the little beach was bliss against the skin. Heat soaked through our sodden boots. Heat rose and wobbled the air above the broom and yellow lupins. We stripped off and spread out our clothes and scooped holes in the warm, moist shingle and rolled around like hippos. Our problems could wait, we figured, and we basked content while Turner manoeuvred the raft to the tail of the sand bar and around the other side. He loosened the rigging and rearranged the packs, which had shifted in the tumbling river. His earlier diffidence had entirely gone, and now he paddled around the raft, lacing everything securely together again and inspecting his handiwork carefully. Finally satisfied, he roused us from our sauna. Leeway, he said. What we want now is leeway.

The island was shaped like a sausage, and close to half a mile long. We dragged the raft to the upstream end, where the river was wider and its flow less concentrated. It was still moving fast, but the opposing shore seemed clear of snags. Turner, with a show of confidence, positioned us strategically around the raft. OK, he said. Swim with the current this time. Don't fight it. There's plenty of room.

It was a textbook trip, compared with the previous shambles. We bounced through the quicker water, kicking hard in mostly the right direction, and hit a pebbly beach like a squad of veteran marines. Turner was pleased. Discipline, he said. Discipline is always the answer. We shook ourselves like spaniels and ran up and down to get dry. Then we sorted our gear and stashed the raft in the bush. We were bulletproof, we could deal with anything. A few minutes away, through an ancient stand of huge, hairy trees, was the El Dorado of the Thomas.

We came out of the timber to a flat, open space of sandy ground, littered with driftwood and the wreckage of washed-up trees. Some were almost buried, and some — the most recent arrivals — still bore living leaves. Small birds were busy in the toetoe at the edge of the bush, and a great flock of pigeons wheeled high in the blue, diving and soaring as if it were springtime. The air was warm and still, with a pleasant boozy smell of growth and decay, of ferns and flowers and the forest floor; and on the far side of the flat, close under a shoulder of cliff, ran the river. It was pale ale in colour when we got close, with a bed of smooth, rounded stones, tawny and wavering in the sunlight. The current

Turner and Two-Pies in the Young — big trout and no other anglers.

flowed evenly through the tail of a pool and into a long, sparkling ripple. It was everything we had hoped for. It was the ultimate dream of a troutstream.

We started up the valley, making good time until Dougal spotted a fish. It was rising, close to the bank, and just above it was another. Turner thought we should keep going till we found the hut, but Dougal wanted to catch one. It's a sitter, he said. We can't just walk past a sitter. He unpacked his gear and rigged up while the sandflies arrived in force. He got himself into position, worked out the line, and dropped a hopper in front of the rearmost fish. It was a nicely-judged cast, the fly settling on the water well enough, and drifting down, drag-free. The trout never hesitated. It bolted, and so did its companion. Nice one Dougal, said Two-Pies.

The valley closed in before long, the river echoing in a deep ravine. The going was good, but strenuous work, with much climbing up and down over the succession of spurs and tributary streams that ribbed the flanks of the Thomas. Two-Pies, who had twisted his ankle, soon fell behind, and Turner started feeling responsible. Don't worry, I told him. He can't get lost, and we'll have a brew ready by the time he gets to the hut. We went on, through gullies of thick bush, up steep, rutted deer tracks onto razorback ridges that skirted the river and opened out, here and there, into easy parklands of well-spaced trees.

The hut stood at the forest's edge, on a terrace above the river at the upstream end of the gorge. It was an old Forest Service structure, solid and basic, with six bunks, a bare food cupboard, and a big, open hearth with a battered metal flue (which didn't work, we were soon to discover, unless the door was left half-open). There was an annex for firewood, also empty, beside the door, and no evidence of recent habitation.

We dumped our packs and walked down to a swathe of deer-cropped grass on a clay bank that dropped straight into the river. The transformation was spectacular. The Thomas slid past in an even flow, more like a canal than a mountain stream. The banks were fringed with low bushes, and the slow-moving water was clear as air. The grey riverbed, several fathoms down, was minutely visible, strewn with a litter of leaves and drifts of silvery shingle, and as far upstream as we could see were the smooth black boles of long-dead trees, jutting from the placid water like the masts of a sunken fleet.

From the bank, almost level with the water, one of these great fossils protruded into the river. It was beer-barrel thick and reached out, submerged, almost halfway to the other side. At the outer end it branched, with the lower fork buried in the mud of the bed and the upper limb leaving a bobbing wake where it projected into the air. Beyond this, slightly upstream, was a good-sized fish.

You saw it first, said Turner.

I went back to the hut for my gear, considering the proposition. I ought to be able to hook this fish. It was a straightforward cast, and it was an innocent, uneducated back-country trout. It was a sitter, or so it seemed — but in fact, as I now realised too late, I had no show of ever landing the thing from such a hopeless position. In every direction, upstream and down, were problems, boltholes, and such a fretwork of intermeshing snags that even making an attempt seemed pointless. Turner would know I was snookered, and would relish the eventual balls-up. It was my own funeral — I should have passed the damned thing on to Dougal.

By the time I was organised Dougal had spotted another one, further out and just as big. We crouched near the edge of the bank and watched them. Nothing disturbed the glaze of the water, and the fish hung almost motionless, swaying gently in position. I knelt in the grass between Dougal and Turner and we swatted the sandflies and debated the options and hoped that something would happen to indicate a workable tactic. Maybe we should just bugger off upstream and leave the problem for Two-Pies.

A cicada flickered out of the bush and crashed into the river fifty yards away. It skittered on the surface, metallic wings vibrating, its iridescent carapace twirling in random, clockwork orbits. The further trout shifted a little to the right and then held still. The cicada motored closer, and the trout, with perfect economy, tilted

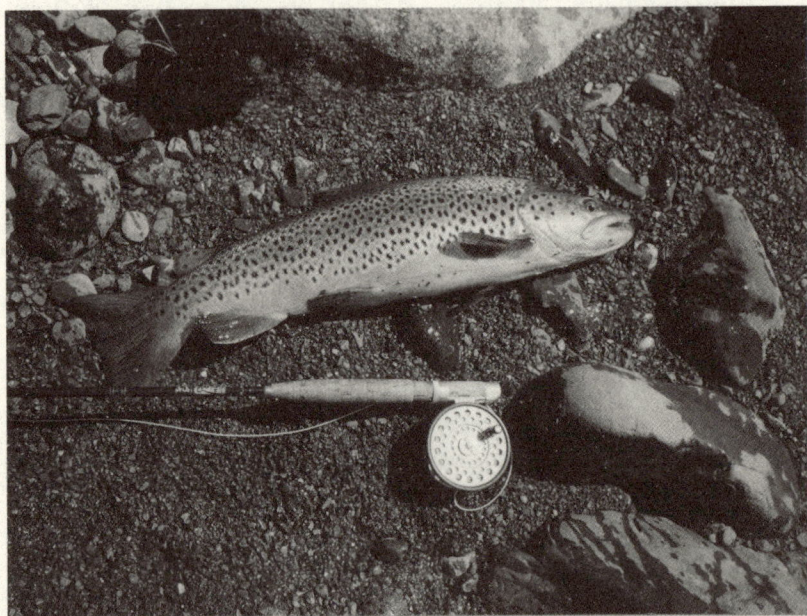

A four-pounder: a decent pair of fillets
and nothing gone to waste.

up and sucked it in. A cluster of bubbles appeared, and popped, and the surface healed, revealing the trout again. Dougal grinned. Now you know, said Turner.

I didn't have a cicada. But I had a fat, red fly, size ten with a deerhair tail, a round-bodied mouthful that I figured would do. I aimed the first cast up the bank, well away from the fish. Not too bad. I stripped more line and shot it out and the fly settled neatly in the middle of the river, an orange glob, nothing like a cicada. Down it drifted, riding high, close enough to the target. No sign of recognition.

You need to twitch it, said Turner.

You need a cicada, said Dougal.

Next float was a classic: dead-on, tiny splash, and sailing on a perfect line. No ignoring this one.

The fish moved sideways. It drifted up and levelled out, just under the fly, the surface still immaculate. It stayed there, sliding back, keeping perfect formation. Please, trout; do it. Just this once. Moments ticked. We stopped breathing. The trout's nose came out, and its whole body rolled over the spot where the fly had been.

I raised the rod and the line came tight and the trout flew vertically upwards, entirely out of the water. It splashed back and angled down, the leader cutting a ribbon of wake. Attaboy, said Turner, pumping his arm in encouragement. The fish was going like a bullet, but it was going in the right direction. It slowed and stopped near the far side, thrashed a few times on the top, and then burrowed under the bank. I could see no obvious snags at this spot, but it only takes one, so I put on a bit more pressure. The fish bellied out of the bank in a puff of mud, gave way a little, and then came racing downstream and across towards me, much faster than I could deal with. It jumped, out in the middle, shot deep again and kept coming, towing a loop of the ballooning line round the fork of the sunken tree. Then, within reach of liberty, it turned around, faced upriver, and stopped.

This was an interesting situation. The fish was now directly below where we stood, and only a rod's length out from the bank. There was no possibility of getting behind it — a mess of snags. There was no possibility, in fact, of going anywhere. I was stuck more or less where I was, with the fish parked in full view, halfway between the surface and the riverbed. I could see the slight pumping of its gill-covers, and the fly in the hinge of its jaw. It looked bigger now, close up, and surely it was able to see me. I took a few cautious steps and it still didn't move. Maybe it was stuffed. Maybe it was just hanging there in the lee of the log, too buggered to go any further.

I gave the rod to Turner and stripped off my jeans and shirt. The sandflies homed in on my pallid Irish skin as I pulled my boots back on again. There was a narrow ledge near the bottom of the bank where the tree emerged, and I slid down and got a footing and Turner passed me the rod. The water came up to my knees at first, and got deeper as I moved out along the log, feet splayed, bow-legged. My shoulders and back were black with flies.

I got past the trout, which stayed where it was. I could hear Turner, up on the bank, saying I don't believe this. I waded further out to where the trunk forked and then carefully squatted until my head went under and my legs were straddling the log. Everything was blurry, but I could see the outline of the log, and then its fork, and I shoved the butt end of the rod down through the angle. It was tricky, because I had to grip the rounded trunk with my knees and pull my torso far enough down to reach around and get a hold of the butt. It didn't work the first time on account of shortage of air.

But the next time I knew what I was doing and I caught the butt and pulled the whole rod through and got back semi-upright again with my head out of the water. I was so cold by this time that I hardly noticed the return of the sandflies.

There was no chance of turning round on the slippery trunk, so I wound in some of the slack and shuffled backwards until I was close enough to shore to throw the rod to Turner. I hauled myself back up and away from the bank and started pulling my clothes on, mashing a red poultice of bloated flies between my shirt and skin.

I was just about dressed and ready to go again when the damned trout finally came out of its reverie and powered off, up and across the river, the line now heading straight for the aerial part of the tree trunk. Well, that was it: bugger the trout. No more submersions for me. But Turner raised the rod high above his head and stood on tiptoe and the speeding line carved its thin wafer of spray and missed the top of the snag by an inch. He grinned around, pleased with himself, and handed me back the rod.

Your fish, he said.

The rest was amazingly easy. The dumb trout got to the far bank, jumped some more, and stayed where it was, a rolling boil on the surface. I horsed it back — a long way — and Dougal got down on the little ledge and flopped on top of it and pinned it under his chest. He worked his fingers through its gills and banged its head with a round pebble, and held it up. It was a lovely fish, a six-pounder with ebony back and red-dotted, golden flanks. We held it up and admired it and took photos. The sun sailed hot in a perfection of sky. Life had seldom been better.

Two-Pies staggered in about mid-afternoon. He was injured, he said. He had fallen and cracked some ribs. But he brightened up when he saw the trout and had a mug of tea and a biscuit. It was a nice trout, he conceded, although it wasn't quite in the monster category. He would get a real monster tomorrow, never fear, but he was going no further today. He picked the best bunk and announced he was having a lie-down. We need firewood, he said.

Firewood turned out to be a hassle. There were a few sodden deadfalls near the hut, but dry stuff was hard to find. The soft, warm air and pillared light within the bush were illusory. This was West Coast bush, an abode of rain, and the forest floor was a moss-deep carpet of humid disintegration. Trees fell, and rotted swiftly.

Fungus devoured the hardest timber. The hut axe was blunt, too, and there was no file, so it took three hours to drag enough fresh-fallen logs and branches down from the ridges and break them apart and stack up a decent supply. After that we decided it was too late to do any more fishing. It had been a great day — with an even better one in store tomorrow. What we needed was a roaring fire and a big feed and a long relaxed evening of companionable bullshit. We were in the fabled Thomas and we had caught a trout — the first, we were sure, of many.

Morning. The fire was dead and the air was cold. Mice were scratching among the billies on the hearth, and Two-Pies was reluctant to get up. He had been attacked by vermin all night long, he said, and pieces had been bitten out of him. Spiders and chiggers were the least of it. The wounds were painful, and they were swelling up exactly like a dire disease he had read about in *Scientific American*. Turner gave him an aspirin and we tipped him out of his bag. Outside was a world awakening to the sweet song of tui and bell-bird, morning mist low on the river, and the breathtaking green of the forest. Today was going to be the day.

There was a vestigial track, skirting the canal-like, log-spiked reach of river that started next to the hut, and we followed this upstream until, after ten minutes or so, it angled back and came close to the river again. This was more like it. This was the Thomas we had imagined: swift bouncy water with fishy depths, silt-bottomed pools, pebbly beaches and fern-hung banks. No swamps — the curse of West Coast rivers — and easy travelling on a perfumed carpet of dried-out sphagnum on the floor of the airy forest.

We snuck along, scanning a succession of classic pools and the faster water between them. There were fresh deer-slots in the damp sand, but no bootprints, no sign or imprint of humanity. It was as if the whole valley were a new creation, and by some fine providence it was ours alone, and the world beyond was no longer accountable.

Noon came and we had seen no trout. The river ran on through forest and glade, ripple and pool, but strangely fishless. Dougal reckoned they were hiding. They're resting, he said. Big, back-country trout are like that. They need to rest — especially in weather as warm as this. They get a bellyful of beetles during the night and park up until they digest them. Don't worry, said Dougal, they'll come on again — it's just a matter of time. He put on a lurid, tinselly fly and waded across a thigh-deep chute to the better side of a long reach that swept in a curving alleyway through a great bench of kahikatea. He worked upstream, covering the water methodically, drifting the fly along the undercut bank and over shadowy crevices in the cryptic riverbed. But the fly sailed unmolested.

We stopped for lunch and a parley. The day was as brilliant as ever, but optimism seemed to be waning. Turner stroked his unkempt beard and aimlessly booted pebbles. This is no good, he said, and I can't see it getting any better. We've been going for nearly four hours over well-nigh perfect water — and if there were trout here we'd have seen them by now. They're not bloody-well resting. They're not parked up. They're just not bloody-well here. These trout don't exist. And we're wasting time — why don't we go back down and try to nail another one of those big buggers we saw yesterday?

Dougal agreed. He had changed his mind, and the upper river, he now concluded, was sterile. It was a mystery, he said. But mysteries occur, as every fisherman knows, and there was no point in arguing with the facts of nature. Turner had the right idea — it was still early in the day, and there might be any number of two-figure submarines, right now, cruising around in the log-filled water above the hut. If we walked fast and stayed on the track we could be back there in less than an hour. Let's get going, said Turner.

Two-Pies, convalescing in a clump of flax, rolled over and

stood up, moaning. I think I've punctured a lung, he said. Maybe both lungs — there's air escaping somewhere. I could die, you know — I could get some kind of embolism or terminal raging infection. I've read about it. But you bastards don't care, do you? I need medical attention. I need a lie-down and a cup of tea. Fuck the Thomas. He glared around accusingly, and, followed by Turner and Dougal, lurched off into the bush.

I let them go, and went on upstream, far from convinced about this ultimate absence of trout. If they had fought their way through the Thomas gorge — the only real barrier on the river — why would they not continue, with such idyllic habitat ahead of them? It made no sense. Harker had told me there were fish right into the headwaters. He had shot one, he said, in a tiny pool by a big slip where the river split into equal-sized tributaries. We had not reached anywhere like that.

The valley continued in an easy gradient, with the hills falling back and the tall bush giving way to smaller stuff and the river a vision in the sun. The sequence of fast water and deep pools continued also, with enticing gutters in the dappled bed, and little eddies of silvery sand where the current boiled out of the rapids. It was amazingly fishy water.

And there were fish alright. The first one I found was sitting just where it ought to be, in a lazy eddy right at the head of a pool. It was a monster, a genuine monster. It was maybe a ten-pounder, and I watched for a long time in case this was the only chance I was going to get. Not that I could see any problems: the fish was rising time after time, scoffing a prolific drift of big, brightly coloured morsels that at first I thought were hoppers. They were translucent and green, with elongated bodies, about the shape and size of a cigarette, and it took me a while to realise that despite their oversize scale and startling colour these were stream-born insects. They were giant stoneflies — the biggest stoneflies ever.

I put on a Muddler Minnow. It looked nothing like the stoneflies, but there were still all sorts of big terrestrials around, and all it would take, I figured, was an oversize fly and a single, well-placed cast.

There was a strip of beach along the side of the pool, unobstructed in front and behind. The trout was rising in clear water about waist-deep, with no sign of dragging currents. Everything was just about perfect — not a breath of wind, and, best of all when dealing with a monster, no jury of spectators. I lengthened the line well off to one side and dropped the Muddler, with a tiny plop, perfectly in position. The monster finned slowly towards it, veered away just short, and bolted, leaving a double wake across the pool. The next three fish were more-or-less repeat performances.

I had gone a long way, further than I knew. The sun was low when I started back, and before long it was dark in the bush. A chill wind had come up, and a thin, driving rain that swirled through the trees and blew in my face. The torchlight was failing and I was just about knackered by the time the first whiff of woodsmoke told me I was nearly home. Then there were voices and a low gust of laughter, not far away, and then a shaft of light in the curtain of rain.

There was a party in progress. The door stood open, billowing smoke, and the interior of the hut was lit with the pulsing glow of a stupendous fire that spilled out of the concrete hearth. It was as hot as a stokehole and the air was almost unbreathable. Dougal and Turner were bobbing around, feeding the fire, on each side of a stacked heap of logs that took up the centre of the cabin. Beyond this inferno, raising his tin mug and beaming expansively in seigneurial ease, reclined Two-Pies. They were drinking black tea with whisky, and an elaborate dinner was roasting and bubbling in camp ovens and pans arranged round the rim of the fire.

They were pleased to see me — and more pleased still when I told them I had caught no fish. Neither had they, so in that regard we were even. They had a new agenda, starting tomorrow. The Thomas had been nothing but a delusion, a silly myth, a blown-up yarn, right from the very beginning — and I should have known better than to believe the crap I had heard from that bullshitting bastard Harker.

Two-Pies was transformed. He was established on the end of his mildewed bunk, close to the flames, his bare chest streaked with dirt and sweat, his broken bones forgotten. He was euphorically drunk and so were the others. He swept a pile of clothes aside to make room on the mattress beside him. This is the life, he said, handing me his mug and retrieving a bottle from the floor. The Thomas is a dog, he said. As we are all agreed. A dismal certified shithole. But this has been an epic trip — an indispensable trip — an experience not to be missed. He flashed me a wide foolish grin and sloshed out a ration of Irish. Yes indeed, he continued: I am glad I came. I have learned things, you see, essential things concerning my life as an angler. I have been injured — gravely injured — but I have discovered how to rely on myself. He beamed generously around the hut. There are great days ahead for all of us. Great days, starting tomorrow. But bugger the Thomas, enough is enough. It is time now to fuck off.

Dinner was a feast, for there was no point in lugging surplus food back to civilisation. We had eggs and sausages and fat rashers of bacon, and plates heaped with carrots and onions and baby peas. There was a chocolate pudding in its own boilable tin, and rice with cream, topped off with honey. The wind whimpered at the window frames and around the eaves, as fresh plans were argued and settled and a hard rain rattled the metal roof. How little we need to defy the elements. Tea and whisky in a tin mug: friendship and disputation.

It was still raining in the morning as we started down the valley. The Thomas was up and rising, its colour a deeper green. The bush was saturated, and soon we were soaked to the skin. In the head of the first gully stood a young hind, ears focused, stock-still, watching. She half-turned, then hesitated, uncertain, and then bounded up onto the ridge and along the track and out of sight. Her scent hung in the humid air.

All thoughts of a swift return to the happy land east of the Alps were cancelled at our first glimpse of the Haast. It had become a mini-Amazon. The scrublands and gravel bars were gone, and the little island had vanished, its warm sands a distant memory. The far shore was obliterated and a grey tide covered everything, and from beneath the cliff where we stood bemused came the rumble of boulders in motion.

There was nothing we could do. We shouldered our weary packs again and started back up the Thomas. The side-creeks were high and hard to cross, and it took more than three hours to reach the hut. We lit the fire and boiled the billy, and hung our wrung-out clothes on makeshift racks. We were almost out of food — another lesson learnt too late — and Turner now reckoned it might be a week before we could cross the Haast.

With no whisky left there wasn't much to do except roll a cigar and read the hut's old magazines and listen to the rain on the roof. Dougal and Turner went out in search of firewood, and in the afternoon I took the rifle and went up the track to look for meat. It was lousy weather for hunting, but about half an hour above the hut, where the big trees started, I found a deer. It was standing on the track, its head stooped in a low clump of scrub and its body nearly broadside to me. It was an easy shot, but to make no mistake I sat down in the muck of the track and braced the rifle with my elbows propped on my knees. I centred the scope and squeezed the trigger and the impact of the .308 slug blew a shining nimbus of atomised moisture from the animal's waterlogged coat. It reared up and spun and took off into the bush. It was hit in the chest. It would go for a hundred yards at the most, then falter and fall.

I walked down the track and found the fresh-churned mud of the hoofprints. I could see the direction the deer had gone, and a few wet traces of blood. But I never found it, despite an hour's methodical searching. Turner was right. There was a jinx on this trip. Nothing was working as it ought to.

It was less than jolly in the hut that night. We were on short rations, apportioned by Turner. But there was one piece of good news. A helicopter had come up the valley, flying very low, looking for deer, and the boys had flagged it down and made arrangements for a jetboat to pick us up at the Thomas confluence at two o'clock the next day. We kept a smoky fire going and had boiled rice for dinner, with butter and salt and the last can of tomatoes, and Dougal produced a big bar of chocolate he had been hiding for emergencies. Conversation ran out early, and when the fire died and the chocolate was gone we went to bed and tried to sleep.

No breakfast. It had rained all night and the creeks were spilling through the bush as we worked our way down the valley. It was far too early for the jetboat, but Turner was in sergeant-major mode. The message might get garbled, he said. You know these chopper pilots. And if we're not there when the boat arrives they'll bugger off. And then we'll be stuffed. Really stuffed, he repeated.

All that day we hung around on the shore near the mouth

of the Thomas, trying to stay warm in the rain. The Haast was bigger than ever, and the Thomas itself was scary, filling its gorge and invading the surrounding forest. Sometimes an entire tree would wheel out of the tide, roots, trunk, branches and leaves thrust briefly aloft, tumbling end over end, and gone. The sky was low and dark above the hiss and rumble of the river. Two o'clock came and went, then three, then four. No jetboat.

We were pushing our luck. It was near five o'clock when Turner decided we would have to retreat up the valley. It was already dim in the bush and some of the creeks were dangerous. Some of them were impossible, and we were forced to climb up the lateral ridges to find a deadfall bridge or a logjam. Two-Pies, who had fallen again and broken more bones, finally balked at crossing a skinny log, high above the creek, with an upright branch right in the middle. Turner and I got around it alright, but Two-Pies refused. He stood on the far bank with Dougal, bawling inaudibly across at us. He pointed upstream, and then they made off into the trees.

Turner was grim. He was responsible, he thought, and the idea of splitting up was a worry. We'll have to go back, he said. We'll never find those clowns again if we don't.

The light was failing rapidly, and Turner was right, but I didn't fancy being responsible. I wanted to be back in the hut, out of the rain, out of this cold, drenching misery. The best thing, I deviously explained, would be for us to keep going as fast as we could. Then we could light a fire, and get a brew going, and have the place nice and warm when the boys showed up. They know what they're doing. They'll be alright. And anyway, I said, I'm not going back over that fucking log.

We cut down through the bush towards the main river and found the track again. But soon we hit another side-creek — the last one before the hut. It was in a narrow defile cut into the rubble and stones of an open, tussocky clearing, and it was churning along chock-full of brown foam and debris. It looked deep from the set of the banks and at the end of the clearing it went over a bedrock ledge and dropped straight into the Thomas. I don't like it, I said.

But Turner thought we could get over. One good lunge into the current and you'd be gripping the opposite bank, he said. And it's probably no better further up anyway. We can make it alright — just don't think about the Thomas. He lowered himself into the water, which came above his waist. I held onto the top of his pack as he leaned upstream, testing the flow. Then he launched out and his pack went under and he grabbed for a massive boulder that stuck out of the other side. He gained it and was swept around, partially into the lee of the boulder. He was up to his shoulders by this stage, but the current was less direct and he was able to haul himself up the steep wall of rubble and out onto the tussock.

My turn, and I still didn't like it. I got into the water at the same place, while Turner dumped his pack and lay down opposite and reached as far as he could out towards me. There was no point in waiting so I shoved off. The water hit me in the chest like a shovel. It filled my eyes and nearly blinded me, knocking me sideways and slamming me against the protruding curve of the boulder. I got a grip and held on, pressed like a limpet against the rock. I saw Turner above me, reaching towards me, and then, slowly, slowly, the huge boulder began to move. The torrent had loosened it and now it was falling, taking me with it. I let go and at that moment felt Turner grasp my flailing left hand. The rock shifted further, falling and rotating at the same time, and then it came away altogether, toppling and vanishing and leaving me in a swirling hole with Turner still above me, still gripping my hand. He held me against the raw rubble like a sack of wet grain while I scrabbled with my boots and he got a grip on both my wrists and dragged me up over the lip of the trench.

It was the final barrier, and we were over. We stood in the rain in the dying day and looked at the gap where the boulder had been. Turner heaved on his pack. It was a good thing, he said, that that bugger turned sideways.

The light was gone in the bush, and we covered the last bit by torchlight, losing the track and pawing our way through blind entanglements of waterlogged undergrowth. Starting a fire took ages. The kindling was wet, and we tore up most of the remaining supply of old hunting and fishing magazines. The damp twigs caught in the end and I built up the flames and made a brew with the last of our tea. The fire grew and we stripped and put on spare clothes, and once we were comfortable I explained to Turner that my life henceforth, by long-held custom, was his concern and responsibility. The only way he could have avoided this fate, I said, would have been to let me go down the creek and into the no-hope of the Thomas. He looked at me strangely and asked if I had banged my head. But he knew what I meant, for we had often discussed the consequences of saving lives.

Turner was quiet for a while. He sipped his brew and studied the fire's red intricacies. Well, I don't know, he finally said; you might have got out of the creek by yourself, without my help. Have you thought about that, by any chance? But he knew he was caught — that without his urging I would never have got into that sluice of a creek in the first place.

When the tea was finished Turner said we would have to search for Two-Pies and Dougal. There was no point in this, as we both well knew, but he seemed to think it was his fault the way things had gone wrong, and he would have to do something about it. He figured they might have got over the creeks but become stuck somewhere up on the side of the mountain. Maybe their torches had run out. Maybe they weren't very far away. He pulled his soaked Swanndri on over his last dry oddments and put new batteries in his pockets and went out into the night.

We had no food left, and no tea either, and once Turner had gone I dug around behind the last old magazines in the cupboard and found some rice in a squashed cardboard box, and a round tin half-full of tea leaves. There was a jar of plum jam, nearly full, with a scab of green mould on top. The rice was well mixed with mouse droppings, and the tea had a whole mouse, sitting up, mummified. I put this haul on the tabletop and spread the rice out on sheets of magazine pages and began picking out the mouse turds one by one. It was pretty easy, although less than entirely one hundred per cent because most of the turds were

Turner crossing a side-creek.

old and crumbly. When I had done all I could I started on the tea, but this was a waste of time. Apart from a few shiny new ones the mouse turds and tea looked exactly the same, so I put the whole lot back in the can and scraped the mould off the jam and built up the fire with two billies of water hung in the middle.

Turner came in not long after. He had blundered around in a circle and ended up back at the door. He was more guilt-stricken than ever and moaned a bit when I told him to stop fretting and have some nice fresh tea. A night in the bush is no big deal, I assured him. It had happened to all of us, and was only to be expected now and again in country like this. The boys will be back in the morning. They'll be wet and buggered and we won't, and that means we made the right decision. I filled our mugs with muscular tea and spooned out the rice and laid on a good topping of sweet plum jam, and Turner got out of his crappy clothes and scoffed it up like a gannet.

The fire smouldered all through the night, holding most of the mosquitoes in the chimney, and I slept oblivious in my decaying bunk, safe from the rain, food in my belly, body and mind untroubled. It was just on dawn when the door banged open and the castaways fell into the hut.

It took a while to make any sense. They were incoherent, mud-slathered and shambling, their wide vacant eyes and wan grey faces alarming. They had climbed a long way up through the bush when they left us, and got over the first creek, but the second one was death and when it grew dark they found a hollow in a bower of pungas and lined it with branches and fronds and crawled into their sleeping bags and lay down on top. The branches sank and the mud rose and the rain finished off the job. But there was no point in moving, so they stayed huddling sleepless in the creeping muck until the first dismal glimmer of day leaked through the pungas.

But at least they were back, and Turner was rapt, delivered from the needle of his conscience. He was up and busy. He stripped Two-Pies to his grimy pelt and put him in his own warm bed. He dug hot embers out of the ash and primed them with twigs and blew the fire back into a blaze. He gave my dry clothes to Dougal, never mind the mud, and kicked me out to go down to the river for water, and in less than an hour the food was cooked and Two-Pies was sitting up, eating plum jam and rice, farting contentedly in Turner's bag and drinking pint after pint of tea.

It was a brief respite. If the boat came today we would have to be there.

We closed the door of the hut for the last time and went into the track through the trees. The lie of the ridges was familiar now, some swaddled in head-high growth, some spaced with great trunks where the track rose and fell and our feet snagged in the criss-cross of roots. A cold rain kept us company, and the eternal wind swirled in the treetops. Water oozed from the earth, pooling in the hollows and dripping from the leaves, and within minutes we were wet to the skin. The side-creeks were full, but we stayed close together and climbed the logjams and deadfalls with the feral confidence of forest animals. In truth we were almost animals now, at home in the bush, moving in accord, as if the journey itself through the grey ribs of the hills were its own guarantee of deliverance. Time passed unnoticed.

There was still no boat when we reached the Haast. We stayed on the shore, constantly moving to fight the cold, listening, watching, waiting. The wind was relentless, driving the rain through our woollen Swanndris, draining our remaining strength. The last heat of the rice had long burned away, and there was no more food. We had burned our energy for nothing.

Turner was as beaten as any of us. All his experience was haunting him now — adventures survived by judgment, or luck, or both. Turner hated inaction, but what could he do? He knew very well that the rain would stop sooner or later, that nothing was permanent, even on the Coast. That the skies would turn blue and the rivers return to their tractable beds — even the monstrous Haast. Until then it was the simple ritual of survival: hunker down, stay warm, stay alive. Food was irrelevant — we could survive without food for a long time. But exposure was a different story.

Turner knew this. His brain could acknowledge it, but all his nature strove against the impotence of our situation. It would soon be dark, and there was only one thing we could do: get into the forest and back to the hut while there was still enough light to make it. Turner knew this, yet he was dithering, pacing the waterline, consulting his watch, peering up and down the river.

He came over, suddenly decisive, and I thought he had come to his senses. He stood in front of us, looking down and shuffling his boots in the pebbles. OK, he said, we can't hang around any longer. We're on our own, so here's what we do. We've still got the air beds. The raft's too heavy, but the air beds aren't. They can sit up high and scoot over the top. He paused to let this intelligence sink in. They're unsinkable, alright? So I'll take one of them and paddle it across. It should be easy enough.

I looked at the river. The wind flicked foam from the tops of its waves, and I thought of the piled-up logs on the old riverbed, and the stands of manuka, now somewhere beneath the surface. A live tree sailed out of the mist, its broken limbs hissing in the surge and vanishing. One snag would sink an air bed. I was cold and miserable, but this scheme was no good. We should be on our way back up to the hut, not colluding in Turner's demise. Things were bound to look better tomorrow. The rain might stop, or I might shoot something to eat, and at least in the hut we would be warm.

No one said anything for a moment, and Turner regarded us quizzically. His thick hair hung like seaweed around his ears and water trickled from his beard. He was bareheaded, eyes narrowed, like a character in some old, mad movie. Captain Scott of the Antarctic, maybe, contemplating extinction and an icy grave. Or

Guy Gibson VC, addressing his heroic crew on the eve of their flight to oblivion.

All objections were futile. Turner's mind was made up. No, he said, we are not going back. Don't worry about it. I'll be across the river in no time. Crank up the car, go down to the village and organise a boat. We should have done it two days ago, before we ran out of tucker. He hoisted his pack and turned away and started up the beach, and we straggled along behind him.

There were two air beds, and it didn't seem fair to let Turner get drowned on his own. Dougal proposed a lottery, but Two-Pies, amazingly, insisted that he was going. He had the old, manic gleam in his eye, and he had had enough of hanging around. The bigger the flood the better, he reckoned. It would spread the waves and fill in the whirlpools, and getting over this lot would be a doddle.

There were no objections from Dougal, and none from me, and it all seemed satisfactorily settled until Turner brought up the matter of Two-Pies' ribs, and nearly derailed the arrangement. But there was no dissuading Two-Pies. His ribs had never felt better, he said. The best possible treatment for busted ribs was lying on top of a lilo.

We dismantled the raft and took the air beds down to a backwater where a creek came into the river. Turner and Two-Pies tried them out, lying on their bellies, legs in the water, holding on to the sides. They kicked around in circles for a practice and then paddled out into the Haast and were swept away, swallowed like matchsticks in the flood.

The rain came in harder, and Dougal and I shifted the packs down near the edge of the water. We walked up and down automatically, although I no longer felt cold. I had stopped shivering some time ago, and had that serene, seductive lassitude that comes at the onset of exposure. I was drowsy and warm, and immune from the rain. I could lie down and rest. I could sleep for a while, right now, right here on the beach. Why continue this wearisome marching? The temptation was overpowering. But I knew what this meant. My body was cooling, not just peripherally, but right to the core — and Dougal, as lightly built as I, must be in the same condition. We had to keep moving. The hut was beyond reach, and we had no option left, and if there was no boat tonight we would never get across the river.

A mallard came over, flying low, and then two more appeared and circled around and landed in a puddle not far from the packs. They were so close I said I could shoot one in the eye and Dougal said OK, do it. I got the rifle and leaned it on the top of a pack and squeezed the trigger. Then Dougal said that we ought to eat the duck — we might be here for a while.

I had a piece of rubber tube and Dougal had half a candle, and we got a little fire going in the lee of a stranded log and put the duck in a billy of water. Dougal knelt in the dirt, blowing into the feeble blaze while I grubbed under deadfalls in the bush, trying to find dry wood. We kept it going for ten minutes or so, but it was a doomed effort and the fire went out before the water was more than lukewarm. But Dougal said there were bubbles on the bottom, which meant it was close to boiling, and therefore the duck was cooked. He let it sit in the billy with the last embers spitting in the rain and then pulled it out and tried to rip off a leg with his teeth. Blood oozed out the corners of his mouth and dribbled down onto his chin.

We left the duck in the billy. At least it had kept us moving. It would be another three hours or so, we figured, before the boys could get across the river and go and organise a boat. But in no time at all there was the sound of a motor. It became louder very quickly and then a small jetboat appeared, fizzing upstream on the crests of the waves and sliding across towards us. It was the cop from Haast, finally alerted, two days late, by the blokes in the helicopter.

He was a young cop, our age, in yellow fisherman's gear and an orange lifejacket. He was very efficient — retrieving people from the backblocks, it seemed, was a regular part of his job. The chopper pilot had told him there were four of us, and Dougal had to explain about Two-Pies and Turner. The cop listened to Dougal and said nothing. He lifted the last pack and set it carefully in the rear of the boat, and gazed back across the river. Lilos, he said. Fucking lilos.

The boat slipped into the current. It tossed around, pointing upstream but moving crabwise like a ferry riding on a wire. The Haast came at us hard, in a weltering flood, opaque and froth-flecked and littered with small islands of vegetation. Trees came past, half-submerged and sometimes several tangled together. Don't worry about trees, the cop said: watch out for half-sunk logs. He worked the throttle, dodging the flotsam, steering round humps and whirlpools. The shoreline grew vague and disappeared and there was no longer a horizon or a point of reference. The boat rose and fell, edging forward, dropping back, and after a time it seemed as if we were stuck in one spot, gunning the motor and then easing off, going nowhere. The wind blew in our faces, spindrift and rain. Grey sky, grey ocean, and then, very close, black rocks in the waves and the streamers of a reef, and beyond it a high dark outline.

The cop edged the boat in closer, skimming lightly between the rocks, and powered through a break in the reef and into calmer water. We were under the bluff, and the next thing Turner was waving and Two-Pies yelling and there was the car, on the edge of the road above. The cop found a backwash at the foot of the cliff, and crept in slowly and kept the motor idling until Turner came down and got in the water and caught the front of the boat. We tossed the packs over in no time and the cop spun around with a snarl of exhaust and blew off into the mist.

It was a slow drive back to the Divide. The rain came down harder than ever and the road was awash. The creeks were roaring and spilling out of the bush, but Two-Pies just went into them, ploughing through hub-high water. Then the wipers broke and slowed us further, but Two-Pies went on, head ducking out the window. He refused to stop at the Gates of Haast, not even for a leak. We are leaving, he said. You can piss all you want when we get out of here. He was gripped with a vision of escape from the Coast, anywhere but the Coast. Warm winds, clear skies, blue streams.

We got to the summit and it was more like sleet. Water was running down the road, humped in a wave in front of the car and sluicing into the bush. The sky was a mystery, the mountains withdrawn, as if something had happened to the clarity of the world while we were in the Thomas. We came round a bend, too fast, and just in front was a deep washout. It was too late to stop. The Datsun sailed through the air and hit the brown, bucking stream about halfway across and sank in a brilliant mushroom of spray and a fandango of collisions beneath the floor. But we kept going from raw momentum and climbed out the other side. The wipers started wiping again.

There was a lake at the first Makarora flat, the little campground submerged and a trestle table floating in the middle of it. The big river was a rolling dark line at the edge of the lake, but the bridge was still intact, and Two-Pies scented freedom. He punched the buttons of the stereo. The Rolling Stones. Mick Jagger. Paint it Black.

We could see further now. We were out of the forest and there were stands of manuka and scattered scrub and the beginnings of open country. The first fenceposts appeared and marched alongside, and the wet earth was spiked with matagouri and the pale skeletons of thistles. The drizzle was thinning, and there was expansion, distance, the reawakening of life. Small sheep stood hunched in the bracken beside the road, and a hawk flapped up from a yellow roadsign, and far away, in the low-hanging mist, shone a splinter of steely light. Two-Pies drove on, exalted, gravel spinning from his wheels. Colour was distilling out of the air, returning to the world, the slashed ochre of tussock grass, the remembered green of pasture. Then the sky lightened like the smashing of a spell, and the clouds blew away, and we rolled out into the sun.

TWO

Tiger

It is nearly the end of the season, and the morning is cool, calm, mellow, the poplars turning golden in the glorious dying of their leaves. There might be time, before Two-Pies arrives, for a second cup of coffee.

Filling the jug I glance across the paddock towards the orchard. A rabbit parts the dew-laden grass to nibble at the shorter turf around the base of an apple tree. There are too many rabbits at the moment, so I fetch the .22 and shoot it from the sill of the kitchen window. There may be another one, so I leave the window open.

Two-Pies arrives, with a valid excuse. He was forced, he says, to drink most of a bottle of Ballantine's at a party the previous night. Couldn't get out of it, he says: fatal to his mana. Yes, he says, dropping into a chair, he'll have a cup of coffee. Back to the bench and refill the jug. We're late already, and it will be lunchtime, now, before we get to the river.

A shadow moves at the base of the hedge — maybe another rabbit. Chamber a round and through the four-power scope the shadow sharpens into the image of a brown-and-yellow cat. It's moving slowly, looking right and left, heading towards the henhouse. It pauses, looking straight at me, straight at the kitchen window — the least movement now, the blink of an eye, and the crosshairs will be empty. But the window is already open, the rifle already aimed, and not even the surgical vision of a cat can detect the microscopic shift of an index finger at a distance of thirty yards. It drops exactly where it stood, translated to feline heaven.

The willow trees form a yellow avenue along the morning highway. Yellow is the colour of happiness; yellow is the colour of autumn. 'Yellow is the colour of my true love's hair,' sings Two-Pies, 'In the morning . . . in the morning.' There's not a breath in the air, not a cloud in the wonderful emptiness of the sky above our dreams of the fishing soon to come.

The river is drifted with fallen leaves. They lie in rafts in the shallows, and turn in the current and impale on our flies. The river is beautiful, but providing no hint of its complex, latent vitality. No flycatchers foray from the silent bush, and a last pair of welcome swallows, tardy in their migration, have given up searching for mayflies and are dicing with the gleaming meniscus of the water, towering high, then vertically back to within millimetres of a ducking. The ripples are empty, and have been for the last three hours, although somewhere upstream Two-Pies is still exploring, still convinced he can beat the odds. The air is balmy, summer-

Two-Pies, Upper Mataura.

warm, and the grass on the flats retains a summer sheen, but fishing is clearly futile in this strange absence of insect life. There are fingers of mist in the gullies, and high cloud moving slowly up from Southland. The weather is about to change.

The river is sterile. It is playing dead. Yet among the rocks of the riverbed are the larvae of millions of mayflies. They are feeding, moving, grazing unseen, their cryptic existences remote from our understanding. They remain submerged for two precarious years, weathering floods, harvesting algae, sheltering beneath the stones. They respond to unseen stimuli, drifting in the flow, burrowing deep, emerging, almost always, with a clockwork predictability. This year, on the Upper Mataura, they have seldom emerged at all.

There is a place ahead where the river pools against a great, black cliff and boils up, fathoms deep. The pool itself, an arena of upwellings and undertows, is difficult to fish, but where it pours out into a smooth-surfaced glide there is good holding water and often there are fish, even when things are slow. And yes, there's a rise. And another one.

A few mayflies are emerging, visible in shafts of sunlight. Trout are rising where there were no trout — at the tail of the pool and along the length of the glide. Chaffinches are suddenly busy and the swallows jink in ecstasy. In the space of a moment, by some hidden cue, everything is different.

It always appears so easy in the growing intensity of a hatch. There are the elfin mayflies, sailing, twirling, perfectly poised, flexing their novel wings. Trout are rolling, shoulders visible, rings on the water mere yards away, oblivious. But nothing is coming to my fly, even though it seems identical to the naturals. Try a smaller one, and it's still the same, still no response.

Another cast, and another. Repeated casts, all futile — until the fly becomes waterlogged and sinks and is instantly seized by a silvery two-pounder. It jumps once and runs towards me, and beaches itself, and I whack it with a bit of driftwood. It is obvious now. The fish are taking nymphs at the point of hatching, and what I need is a half-drowned fly, something that will barely float.

Fingers fumbling, and the knot pulls out as I tighten it. Trout are plopping all around — it is, as the old books say, a stern test of the angler's sang-froid. I manage the knot in the end and make a cast. An instant boil, a well-timed strike — and a lovely multicoloured jack leaps high above the water. It powers off, downstream, through a boulder run, and into the next big pool, still leaping. I follow, ploughing through the gorse, but the leader parts.

Ten minutes, and it's all over. The river has gone to sleep again: not a solitary, vagrant rise. Visibly unchanged, everything has changed, but it doesn't matter — one fish on the bank is enough. Two-Pies appears and wades across, his face a cipher of contentment. I got four, he says. Monsters. You wouldn't believe it.

The fire in the hut glows companionably with a crackling of macrocarpa. The dinner is cooking: fallow venison in bacon fat, onions, garlic and peas. A tall glass of Guinness, creamy cool, in the warmth of the homely light. It may rain tomorrow, but the high cloud has passed without effect, and the forecast may have been wrong. We are endlessly optimistic, all of us who fish for trout.

Two-Pies looms in the doorway. That cat, he says. You know — Ray and Denise's cat — the big black one.

Yes.

Well, he grins. Bad news. It's just gone down the road with your take-home trout.

THREE

The Backwater

The backwater was several years old and already overgrown. A wall of ancient willow trees lined one former bank, and a thicket of new growth was sprouting from the mud of what had once been part of the streambed. It was fed by an underground flow from the main channel, now some distance away, and drained by a deep gutter lined with watercress.

There were five or six trout in the backwater, all of them big, aggressive fish, intolerant of their neighbours, but able to co-exist, more or less, in the spreading cover of an interlinked series of willow-shaded bays.

The fish patrolled unhurriedly, fins hardly moving, quickening only at the sight of a floating willow-grub or the proximity of a rival. But there were plenty of willow-grubs and plenty of confident rises, and had this been a normal stretch of the open river I would have said these trout were easy meat.

But it wasn't going to be anywhere nearly that straightforward. They were big fish, for a start — a good deal bigger than the two-and-a-half-pound average for this section of the Mataura. They were bigger, older, and therefore, presumably, smarter. If hooked they would surely have the wit to react immediately — denying me that brief willow-grub moment of confusion when more juvenile and innocent fish could often be horsed away from the snags and into the middle of the stream. These brutes would never fall for that — and, besides, there was no convenient middle of the stream to horse them into. There was just a maze of connected pools, deep in a matrix of willows. Once hooked, a trout would have to be held exactly where it was, with no chance of following it downstream, upstream, or in any other direction. The prospects did not look good.

I crouched in the thick scrub and watched, trying to think of a workable tactic. Four-pounders slid past in a regular sequence, timed, it seemed, to minimise the possibility of confrontation. Now and again this protocol failed, and a brief tail-chase ensued, establishing the pecking order. But these displays seemed mostly perfunctory, as though the trout understood that the water was shallow and the bottom was mud and any excessive pyrotechnics would stir it up and end the picnic for aggressor and aggressed alike.

What I needed, I decided, was a massive fly with a heavy hook and a leader thick enough to dispense with the usual niceties. This was no place for decorum. This would have to be brutal, with the trout hooked, played and landed in one almighty heave.

I selected a deer-hair cicada, and matched it to a nine-pound tippet — far from elegant, but pretty close to unbreakable. I smashed a hole in the branches up behind me, sufficient for a minimal back-cast, and lobbed my killer into position. A trout arrived almost immediately. It speeded up, heading straight for the cicada. This is it, I thought: this is going to be a pushover.

The trout came closer and pivoted, its pectoral fins back-pedalling. Its nose emerged, its big jaw opened, and it picked an almost invisible willow-grub from the surface film alongside my cicada. Then it moved slightly to the left, and scooped up a couple more. The cicada, a gross no-hoper, rocked impotently in the backwash, its nine-pound nylon hawser printing a fat shadow on the bottom. Plan A was definitely kaput: it was willow-grubs or nothing and I'd have to take my chances with the leader.

I retrieved the cicada and inspected my arsenal of grubs. The Mark Ten, my latest, should do the trick. It looked even better than the naturals, so I tied one on and got it into the air. The back-cast was tricky, and the grub snagged in the willows, too high to reach, and when I jerked it free it shot forward and dropped onto the water in front of me. There were no fish in sight, and I had almost finished winding in the slack line when a four-pounder shot from under the trees and grabbed the grub, which had sunk and was lying on the bottom near my feet. The tiny hook caught briefly, and then pulled away, and the trout, with a dubious wag of its head, cruised on.

The next fish came along within a couple of minutes, and this time I was organised. A Mark Ten was greased and floating properly at the end of a four-pound tippet, out in the deeper water next to the overhanging willows. The fish moved confidently into the pool, heading straight in my direction. It rose, took a natural, and rose again, inhaling my imitation.

I raised the rod-tip sharply, and the trout erupted in a fountain of spray, tumbling end over end. It fell, hit the surface broadside, and jumped out again — even higher this time, water flying everywhere. It made no attempt to get under the willows, which would have been very easy. It just acted as though the water had suddenly become intolerably hot and it had to stay in the air. Up and down it bounced, doing back-flips and barrel-rolls at an altitude of about six feet.

There was nothing to do but keep a straight line and hope that the lunatic fish would keep on jumping until it was totally shagged. If it did this, then maybe I could actually land it, which, considering the odds, really would be something special. So I held on and the trout kept going berserk — bouncing on the one spot like a Christmas kid on his new trampoline. Maybe these big backwater trout were not so clever after all. Maybe . . .

Clouds of mud billowed up and filled the pool, and the surface quickly disappeared beneath a chocolate froth of bubbles. The fish had amazing energy. It jumped higher and higher, and then, with a spectacular effort, it leapt into the lower branches of the willows. Well, that's the end, I thought — gave the bugger too much slack.

The trout was caught on a matted skirt of leaves and branches that reached out across the pool almost level with the surface. It was a solid platform, closely interwoven, and the trout, rather than falling through, was still bouncing. It was staying aloft, foiling its own best chance of escape and keeping the line from snagging. And then, with a couple of powerful somersaults it was back in the pool in front of me.

No trout can leap continuously for more than a very few minutes. This one was extraordinary, but its strength was nearly exhausted, and I held it carefully in the middle of the pool as its marvellous leaps diminished, until finally it was wallowing helplessly on the surface of the churned-up slough. It was utterly spent, and there was no resistance as I grasped the leader and eased it slowly towards me.

Almost at my feet the hook pulled free. The fish made no reaction. Unaware of its liberty it lay in the shallows, its belly and flanks exposed, its gill-covers pumping the muddy water. It was finished, I thought, and I watched it for a moment, and pounced.

My fingers closed across the dark-brown back, and I felt the trout in my grasp. But the sudden contact was galvanic, and with a final surge of energy it twisted and leapt away.

The river was idyllic all through that Indian summer, the mornings moody in skeins of mist, and mayflies hatching at noonday among drifting yellow leaves. Then the weather broke in a plague of storms. Floodwaters scoured the Garvies, the Eyre Mountains, and all the barrier ranges of Southland. Huge trees from distant forests roiled down the swollen waterways and came to rest as splintered wrecks in the middle of lowland paddocks. Bridges, secure for decades, were swept to summary oblivion.

I went back to the Mataura in November, after snowmelt. The river had changed its course again, and the backwater had vanished so completely there was no evidence it had ever existed. A deep, swift glide now ran beneath the limbs of the old, immovable willow trees, but the young growth that had stitched the former shore was entirely swept away. There was a fine ripple at the head of the glide where, less than a year before, had lain the seductive pools of the backwater. I stood on a beach of clean-washed pebbles and caught a two-pounder in the ripple, but it was skinny and I put it back. There was no sign of the bouncing trout.

FOUR

Kevin

In appreciation of Frederick Halford, who fished with nothing but the floating fly. And G. E. M. Skues, his rogue contemporary, who advised us not to be so silly.

Kevin was a shrapnel slinger — or as close to it as makes no difference. He lived in Devonport, and his idea of fishing was to camp at Taupo for a couple of weeks every summer, dredging the riverbeds with fast-sinking lines and tossing banana-sized lures at the lake. He snagged his share of big, eager rainbows, and was happy with the game, imagining that he was fly-fishing.

This serendipity went on for ages, and might have continued indefinitely, had Kevin not read an old book by George Ferris about fishing in the lower South Island. This was a dire shock to Kevin. There was no mention of high-density lines, or treble hooks, or Matukas or Hamill's Killers. Instead there were Twilight Beauties and Greenwell's Glories — tiny flies tied on hooks the size of a match-head. There were floating lines and delicate leaders, and magnificent trout in a universe of streams so perfect and plentiful as to beggar the imagination.

Kevin was distraught. He ransacked the local library and read everything he could find on fishing in Otago and Southland. He discovered nymphs and duns and spinners, and the differences between stoneflies and mayflies. He cancelled his annual trip to Taupo, and stayed at home all summer in a slough of despond, reading furiously and swilling shiraz in the new-found and dismal knowledge that, as a bona fide fly-fisherman, he had hardly even begun.

Things got worse later that year when Kevin, who, between times and among other things, is a poet, bumped into Turner at some kind of poetry knees-up at the university in Auckland. Turner and Kevin both won prizes and, inevitably, they got on the turps — and the conversation, equally inevitably, turned to fishing. It was all quite true, said Turner. The south was a trout arcadia. The rivers were full of them, cunning as cats, powerful as locomotives. Decades of experience were necessary, and even then only the elect could catch them. The flies were practically invisible.

Kevin arrived in mid-November and phoned Turner from the airport. He had two weeks, he said, and he wanted to start immediately. His Taupo gear had been disposed of, and he was irrevocably committed. He would need a new rod and line, and suitable flies — and, of course, transport to the fishing.

I met them in the pub that evening. Kevin was fully rigged out with his brand-new kit, buying rounds, bubbling with happy impatience. They were starting in the morning, and since Kevin was an unknown quantity Turner said it might be best to assume the worst and take him somewhere in range of an easy fish. He had been known to catch rainbows, apparently, so maybe the Ahuriri? We drank a few more jugs and discussed the problem, and by closing time the arrangements had been settled.

The Ahuriri, when we got there, was up and opaque as porridge, so we made a detour to the Birchwood lagoons to let Kevin see some fish. The earlier wind had died, and the water was clear, and every few minutes a big trout would come cruising past. The first one was about twelve pounds and Kevin got so excited he could hardly wipe the steam from his glasses. We let him scare them all away and then drove on up the valley towards the hut, rabbits bouncing in front of us and skittering into the shingle. I shot a couple of young ones and we stewed them in a billy for dinner.

There was low mist along the Ahuriri in the morning, but the tops were bright in the rising sun as we climbed up through the beech forest and scree-slopes to a pass that led into the top of the Dingleburn. Our packs were loaded with food and grog, and Kevin managed remarkably well for a poet and an Aucklander. He fell over and bent an ankle, but he never complained, hobbling down the rough, tussock-clad ridges to the easier going on the floor of the valley. We made a brew in the Top Dingle Hut, and sat outside, our bodies decompressing. Then we went down to the river.

It was the perfect introduction. There were grasshoppers bouncing everywhere and four rainbows frisking around in the first little pool, and Kevin landed two of them. He made huge long casts and put his fly down with a mighty splash each time, but it didn't seem to matter — the fish just raced to nail them. They had probably never seen an angler, and Kevin would have got the lot if he hadn't botched two of the strikes. But he learned quickly, and over the next five days he caught dozens of trout on just two basic flies: the Coch-y-bondhu and the Hare and Copper.

There is only a certain amount you can learn from catching suicidal rainbows. Kevin needed something more challenging, so we went back over the hill to the Ahuriri and drove all the way to the Mataura, and then, after a couple of days, we shifted to the Oreti. Kevin caught more fish, including some really tricky ones, and went back to Auckland happy.

In later years we fished everywhere — all over the lower South

Kevin in his natural habitat.

Island. Kevin became a competent dry-fly man and a lethal exponent of the nymph, and the Hamill's Killers were forgotten, never to be mentioned again. The weather was always fine when Kevin arrived — he had an anti-jinx. The skies cleared, the northerlies calmed, and the rivers murmured in unfailing good humour. And every season the flies got smaller and the leaders longer, and the trout got a good deal smarter — but Kevin still managed to catch them. Kevin caught more than anyone.

One golden day especially remains always in my memory. We were fishing the Mataura, and there were willow leaves in the water, above the bridge at Ardlussa. It was late autumn, but the sun shone in a clear blue sky. The tourists had gone and the river was ours — low, clear, impossibly enticing. It was a day that promised everything — a morning hatch, a spinner fall — but the trout were nowhere to be seen. Nothing animate disturbed the serene sterility of the Mataura. And then — as I knew that eventually it would — a dun appeared on the surface. And then another, and another. Kevin! Kevin, get ready.

There is nothing more magical or exciting than this moment of transition. The river flowing like time itself through a universe unaltered except to the eyes of the hidden trout — and the patient eyes of the angler. The first few drifting, sunlit duns — and then, at the tail of the pool, in the glassy water — the splash of a bold, small fish.

Kevin was up ahead of me, stork-like in a knee-deep glide. A big trout rolled in front of him, a slick bulge on the surface, and Kevin, too close, moved back a bit. Kevin was on the ball.

I crossed the river and searched ahead. There were more and more mayflies lifting away, and several trout were rising. I hooked the first on a Cul de Canard, but it jumped around and came off. The next one was a ripe four-pounder, fat and maternal and unwilling to risk dislodging her eggs in a serious struggle to escape. She conceded the game with little fuss, and swam unhurriedly away after I freed the hook. The slack water at the shingle's edge was a soup of mayfly husks.

The belly of the pool was empty, but there were five or six little fish lined up in a long, roily chute at the top. They were high in the white-streaked water, busy as sparrows at a barbecue, and each of them in turn made a slashing grab for my ragged, half-sunk fly. But none of them were hooked, not even briefly, and the last in line, undeterred by its narrow escape, stayed where it was and kept on feeding. It had learned to avoid the Cul de Canard, but took a Pheasant Tail Nymph and tore off downstream. It was a two-pounder, firm-fleshed, requisitioned for dinner.

Kevin appeared on the far bank, looking a bit pissed off. Things weren't going too well, and he waded over, barking the inevitable question. Yes, certainly, he assured me, there were plenty of fish. Yes, they were rising — frolicking all over the bloody river. But no, he hadn't caught any. He had lost a fly box with all his smallest flies, and was using a grape-sized, fuzzy item, manufactured in Auckland. The fish, of course, were ignoring this, so I gave him what he needed and away he went, looking grimly determined. Autumn hatches don't last long. Kevin was under pressure.

I went through a fortress of late-flowering gorse and around a backwater to a place where I had often caught trout, and, yes, more rings were widening. There were duns on the water, but now spinners as well, rising and descending in the lazy air, and the fish were feeding methodically, holding in place and taking only the flies in their line of drift.

Money cannot buy something like this — an inversion of the settled order of things, in the face of coming winter. Distant stars were in fleeting alignment, and the season, looping back on itself, was playing once more a summer song, in defiance of the falling leaves. The fish fed in primal innocence, their guile erased by this rare, late-season plenty, and I watched each one — watched it quicken and move to my fly, tightening the line, seeing the surface shatter. Time ceased, became irrelevant, before the river returned to itself again, before the witchery ended.

Where was Kevin?

He hadn't come past me so I walked back down to the shingle beach where we were when the hatch had started. No sign. I went on downstream, cutting across the tail of a pool to a high bank where the river curved in a sudden bend and opened out into a broad, two-sided ripple. Sure enough, Kevin was there, his rod tracing the rapid drift of his line, mending and casting and mending again.

He hadn't seen me, so I crept up very close and hunkered under a willow. Kevin is a master of ripples — who knows what I might learn? But he looked up and saw me, and raised his free hand, four fingers showing. I just got here, he said. He was following the floating line as he spoke, throwing a mend, drawing in the slack, and — as if on command — another trout came tumbling out of the river. Kevin held it tight and bounced it ashore. This place is stuffed with the buggers, he said. Use a sixteen black beadhead.

It was an old, immovable ripple, armoured with solid boulders. The far side was still untouched, and I waded across, well downstream, and came up almost level with Kevin. It should have been easy. The sun was low on the western hills, and my line stood out like an artery in the jouncing, coppery water. I worked every seam, for nothing, while Kevin hooked five more fish. He played them with larrikin carelessness, reining them tight, and laughing when two of them came off.

It was some distance to the car. There were stars in the pale sky and the river ran like mercury beneath the dark hedge of the trees. Kevin was happy: the doldrums of his day forgotten, his mana magically restored. But there was still something that I knew was niggling him — something unresolved, still unmentioned.

We walked along a sheep track through the riverside broom and across the rough, stony paddocks. I get bored with the dry fly sometimes, said Kevin at length. Don't you find that? I made no reply — this was likely to be good — and Kevin was quiet for a minute or two, ruminating his spiel. Yes, he continued in a confiding tone, the dry fly is overrated. It's a bit of a fetish, really, this fixation with hatching flies and catching fish on the surface. What's so special about that? Flies jumping around, coming down like bloody confetti. It's all so juvenile and obvious.

Well, maybe, I said. But plenty of people would disagree. Look at Two-Pies. You could hardly say he was a juvenile, but he won't fish with anything else, so how do you account for that?

Kevin freed himself from the top barbs of a fence. He picked up his rod and his net and his line of thought. Ignorance, he said. Prejudice and ponciness and double-dyed incorrigible bloody ignorance. That's all it is in the end. Ignorance. You'd think we'd have learned in a hundred years, but here we are, still stuck in a rut with that old fraudster Halford and his tweedy gang on the bloody Itchen. One-eyed Pomgolian plutocrat. Hah! What did he know about fishing outside his precious chalk stream?

He was pretty good, from what I've read.

Indeed, indeed. But he'd be totally stuffed out here, you know, old Halford. Completely rooted. Not an ounce of imagination. That's the trouble with these dry-fly blowhards. Dry fly, dry fly, dry fly . . . like a kind of tribal mantra. No concept of strategic range, you see. Total lack of adaptability. That's the true measure of an angler — elasticity, an open mind, the . . . the . . .

The ability to change tactics when the chips are down?

That's right. My point exactly. That's what a real angler needs. Not sticking to the same old method no matter what.

No further response was needed. The controversies of a century ago, still viable, had been pressed into service once more, and Kevin was finally satisfied. He flashed his best diabolical grin and strode ahead, indomitable, chuckling to himself in the gloaming.

Kevin is an Aucklander, a different breed, brazen as a bailed-out banker. One day the trout may trip him up, as they usually do. But then maybe not. Maybe Kevin is an exception. If Harry Houdini had been a fly-fisherman Kevin would have left him for dead.

FIVE

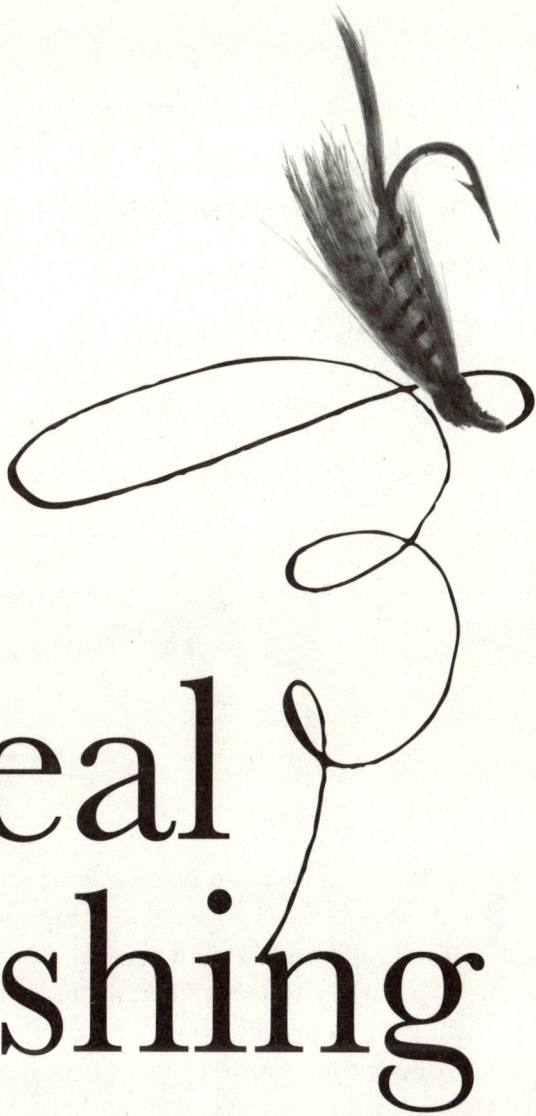

Real
Fishing

A letter this morning. From Mrs Phoebe Zeitgeist, of Blueskin Bay. 'Dear Dave,' she writes (the ink is green, the paper primrose, thick and creamy, a whiff of jacaranda).

'Dear Dave, I have been reading your angling stories for a number of years — ever since my late husband went off a three-hundred-foot vertical waterfall somewhere over on the Coast. He was a very keen fisherman, and I thought that your writing might provide some kind of connection — some key, even — to the outdoor world he loved so much. Unfortunately, however, this has not been the case, and that is why I am writing to you. To be brutally honest, Dave, your stuff has always been pretty bad, and lately has been getting much worse.

'You never seem to talk about real fishing, and mostly you never catch anything, and I can remember one long-winded piece about six months ago where you were supposed to be going fishing but never even got out of the pub. This simply is not good enough. People are paying hard-earned money to read about fishing, and you serve them this kind of drivel. It's disgraceful, actually. And even when you do talk about fishing it isn't exciting enough. It's boring. Why can't you write really thrilling stories like the ones that they have in the Australian and American magazines, with the scream of the reel and so on? Huge monster salmon as big as the boat. Bears, too, if you like.'

OK. That's it. When it comes to comparisons with the Aussies and the Yanks the gloves are definitely off. Cudgels at dawn: no quarter asked or given. Here, then, is the true and unadorned account of the time that Albert and I fished the legendary Grebe River.

We crossed the mountains in a blizzard. Visibility was next to zero at times and we were forced to steer by instinct, up to our necks in snow. We found the pass eventually and tobogganed down on top of our packs to the very edge of the forest. The sky was clearing by then, and very soon the clouds blew away and the great gash of the Grebe valley lay spread before us, bathed in ethereal light. It was not yet noon, and within two hours we were on the valley floor, mired in the endless Grebe Swamp.

All afternoon we travelled through the stinking morass. The pitiless sun blistered about us, and Albert, more heavily burdened than I, occasionally broke through the floating mat of vegetation and vanished into the gurgling abyss below. Many times I thought he was irretrievably lost, but always, somehow, he reappeared, like a mutant, slime-clad amphibian, hauling himself out of the depths. Once he was gone for six minutes.

Here and there in the oozing wilderness we skirted great

dank pools of foetid water inhabited by yellow-eyed eels, six feet or more and agile as alligators. They erupted on the surface, writhing and snapping and gliding alongside, watching us for any stumble. Clouds of mosquitoes attended us, and there were huge dragonflies, purple and gold, and flights of small green chittering birds that they pursued and sometimes caught. It was a place of death and the ancient odour of organic decay.

But in the evening we reached firm ground and easy travelling. The day faded to a velvet night and a full moon rose above the mountains. The silvery tussocks beckoned us on, and by midnight we were roasting before a mighty fire in the Clark Hut. Albert poured generously the Captain Morgan and told me of Archie Clark, a friend of his youth.

Clark had built this hut with a hammer and an adze and a pocketful of nails in 1940, when the rest of mankind was otherwise engaged. He had built it well, too: the scalloped adze-strokes glinting on lintel and beam, the hand-hewn timbers tight and proof. We roasted steak in the open flames and boiled the rice and beans in a cracked camp oven and washed them down with the Captain Morgan. Warm and replete, we toppled into the bunks, and the mice, unmolested, rifled our sodden packs.

It was morning. The din of Albert's breakfast preparations awoke me. The sun shone and the sky was clear and Albert whistled and sang. We ate in an ecstasy of anticipation.

Below the hut was the Jaquiery, a main tributary of the Grebe, emerging from its granite gorge in the western wall of the valley. A sequence of pools and deep channels ran between the gorge and the confluence with the Grebe, and the morning light was fingering the first of these when we reached the water.

Albert was casting, and I sat watching. It was too early, I

thought, but suddenly he stiffened, and I knew there was a fish. The rod leapt upward and bent with the impact of the strike. The reel sang its song as line spun from the whirling spool, and Albert leaned back, trying hard to control that first, mad rush.

The fish made for an undercut cliff, boring deep. We had still not seen it and could only guess its size. A tangle of sunken branches ringed the base of the cliff — once there the fish was lost.

But it was slowing. Albert thumbed the line and dropped the rod-tip level with the water. The fish was stopped. It turned now and ran downstream and back across the pool, slack line piling up, very dangerous.

Albert grunted and reefed slack, running backwards over the shingle, stumbling, yelling and swearing. A splintered log enmeshed his legs, throwing him heavily. Then on his feet again, limping and bloodied, the rod-tip broken but the fish still there. It was racing back across the river now, fighting deep, as strong as ever.

Albert gained line. He followed the fish. He was out in the tailwater, waist-deep, the broken rod hooped double, the fish close but unyielding. For long minutes they remained thus, the fish and the fisherman, motionless.

Sweat poured down Albert's face and chest. Cords of taut muscle ribbed his neck, and his wild rapt eyes glowed like coals. The line hummed and hummed, and then, with a sickening twang, the hook pulled free.

In disbelief I gazed at the scene, and Albert collapsed, heartbroken. Tension gone, the line recoiled over our heads and the fly pinged against a high rock face. And then, by some odd impulse, it flew forward again, and settled in the stream, almost at the place it had emerged. Albert was heedless, his eyes unseeing, his day destroyed.

But the trout was still there, and it turned and seized the fly with a slashing rise. The fight was on again and the fish raging through the pool, waves crashing on the shingle.

I lay back in a tussock and watched. Sometimes the noise of

battle was close to me in the pool, Albert stumbling blindly about, flailing dementedly at the swarms of meat-eating insects that now fastened on his sweat-sweetened flesh. Then he would be away downstream, out of sight, a commotion of rending trees and howls of pain echoing along the river. And then back again, stark naked and black with flies. I could take no more.

In Albert's pack I found the Captain Morgan. There was about a quarter of it left, just enough to fill my enamel mug. The day was warming and a light wind had come up, and I sat cushioned by the pack, half-bemused, sipping the fiery liquid. Insects whirred and attended to their lives, and a small lizard slid out of the grass and climbed over my boot. The grass rustled softly in the breeze, but there was no sound or disturbance from the river, and after a time I forgot about Albert and wandered away from the shingle beach, through the long tussock grass and into the astonishing forest. The air was motionless and cool among the big trees, and in the shady, arrowed light everything became very clear to me. The rocks of the earth rammed through the forest floor. The wind blew and the trees grew and the words that confused me had all gone away.

The sound of the river. The soft lapping of water, and Albert's familiar voice. We were back on the little beach by the pool, and Albert, mud-smeared and bloody and bare, leaned close. 'I put it back,' he said. 'It was undersized — but we need to get going. There's a big one rising about half a mile down. You won't have any bother at all with the bastard.'

SIX

Crocs
& Barras

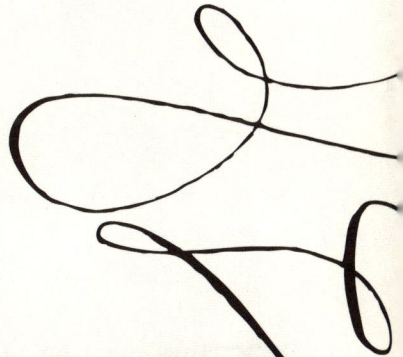

Kevin came down in November, as usual, and before he went back to Auckland he talked me into going fishing in Australia during the winter. To a place called Weipa, in the far north, on the Gulf of Carpentaria.

This was a bit of an odd proposition, because Kevin has never shown much interest in any fish other than trout, but his glowing description of the amazing treats in store persuaded me to agree. I found out later, of course, that he didn't know a damned thing about Weipa, or the kind of fishing we would be doing — that he himself had been conned into it by Two-Pies one evening after a couple of bottles of red, and he wanted me to come along because I, being as ignorant of sea-fishing as he was, would to some extent dilute his anticipated display of incompetence. The other members of the party — Dougal, Randy and Bubble — had been there several times before, along with Two-Pies, and — compared with Kevin and me — were well ahead of the game.

Anyway, having agreed to go, I cornered Dougal in the pub and quizzed him about the prospects. Wonderful, he said. All kinds of fish. Innumerable species, every size and shape — a veritable fly-fishing paradise. It would do me a power of good, he said. Blast me out of my lifelong fixation on trout, and alter my view of everything.

And it wasn't just the fishing. Oh no, it was a whole new way of life. There would be outback adventures from morning to night: near-death encounters with mad buffaloes, crocodiles and giant sharks. Fall off the boat, said Dougal, and you're dead — ripped to bits in seconds.

This was hardly my idea of a restful break from the winter, and Dougal had to backtrack fairly seriously to stop me from phoning Kevin and alerting him as to what he was in for. No, no, no, said Dougal. There was nothing to worry about, really. They had all survived last year, after all, and the death rate from sharks was, statistically, remarkably low — nobody eaten by either a crocodile or a shark since that German skinny-dipper two years ago. And what was a croc expected to do, anyway, in such a situation? Nude lady in a moonlit billabong; it was a scandalous provocation. The poor croc had no choice at all, when you come to think about it. So, don't fret, it's safe as houses.

I wasn't entirely convinced, but it was too late. Kevin had bought the tickets.

It was hot on the tarmac at Weipa, an industrial dormitory built on a bauxite deposit about twice the size of New Zealand. The countryside was flat and covered with grey, nondescript scrub, and the air was hazed with drifting smoke, the product of bushfires that had been burning for years all over this part of northern Queensland. It was hot at the airport and hot on the road, but soon we were in a large, cool bar, gripping pints and discussing the plans for the coming week with a big Australian called Fish, our main guide. The weather had been very settled for the time of year, said Fish — the last cyclone was more than two weeks ago — and angling conditions were excellent, especially for fly-fishing. And, no, there had been no casualties on account of sharks, crocodiles, snakes, or buffaloes — not even a mutilation. We dumped our gear at the beachside lodge, found the bottles of duty-free whisky, and by bedtime that night Weipa was looking good.

In the days that followed I realised that Dougal had been right about Weipa. The waters were prolific beyond belief, and I caught more fish in that brief time than in my entire previous existence. We fished every day, and there was no opportunity for indolence, or simply going fishing when one wanted to — no late nights of sozzled dispute and festering abed till noon. We were out every morning at the glint of dawn, and off to the boats (three boats, three guides, two of us per guide), and away across the still-sleeping ocean.

For the first time in my life I enjoyed the early morning. The air was cool and sweet, and there was a breathless hush on the tropical sea, with no hint yet of the terrific sun and the hot, battering wind, and the fish — the innumerable, unaccountable fish to come.

Saltwater fly-fishing is a wonderful pastime, but it's a stretch to call it fly-fishing. The tackle is similar, apart from the 'flies', but fly-fishing for trout in a New Zealand stream is a universe away from what we were doing at Weipa. There are no flies in the sea. No mayflies, stoneflies or caddis. There are no flies that are relevant to the fish at all, and while definitions have become more elastic in recent years it is still understood by most fly-anglers that a fly should be a fly — or an insect at least — and that sardines, lobsters, small mammals, or snakes, do not, in all conscience, pass for flies. The mere fact of delivering such organisms with a fly-rod does not alter the case, and you are no more fly-fishing when using this kind of artillery than you are playing cricket when beating a pig to death with a bat.

Definitions aside, it was marvellous fishing. The main thing, once the guides had found the fish, was to deliver a big lure somewhere reasonably close. It wasn't very hard, and soon even Kevin and I were hauling them in by the boatload. Tarpon, queenfish, giant herring, cobia, garfish, tuna, shark and several kinds of trevally were among the kaleidoscope of species we encountered, with many of them, pound for pound, far more powerful than trout.

Usually we fished separately, the three boats heading to different destinations each morning, but one day, in search of tuna, we cruised in sight of each other a long way down the coast. For nearly two hours we saw nothing, until a vague dark blob appeared on the sea ahead, which at first I thought was seaweed. But when we got closer it was clearly a living thing, its outermost edges stirring the water in rhythmic undulations. It was a manta ray, said Fish. There would be remoras underneath it, and maybe something catchable, but probably not tuna, so we idled around the great, indifferent island of flesh, and left it undisturbed.

Fish was confident about the tuna. We would find them, he said, and, sure enough, we found them before long, feeding on an enormous shoal of baitfish. It was a classic meatball, ten acres of sardines, dancing out of the water. The whole surface was a foaming vibration of demented sprats, harassed from below by the tuna, and from above by a storm of gulls. We motored up close, almost into the meatball, where the racket was deafening and the air delivering a steady hail of birdshit. Fish had the rods set up with the right lures already attached.

The tuna weren't very big — about twenty to forty pounds — but once hooked they were nearly unstoppable, and any hesitation in getting them on the reel, or an overrun, or kink in the line, and they were gone. It was exhilarating and sometimes frightening on the tiny, flat deck on the bow of the boat, rising and falling on the ocean swell, the rod bent to its limit and the big reel whirling against its tight-wound drag.

The first few fish escaped, but then Bubble got one into his boat, and then Randy did, and then I did. It was simple, really — just fire the lure far enough in the right direction, let it sink

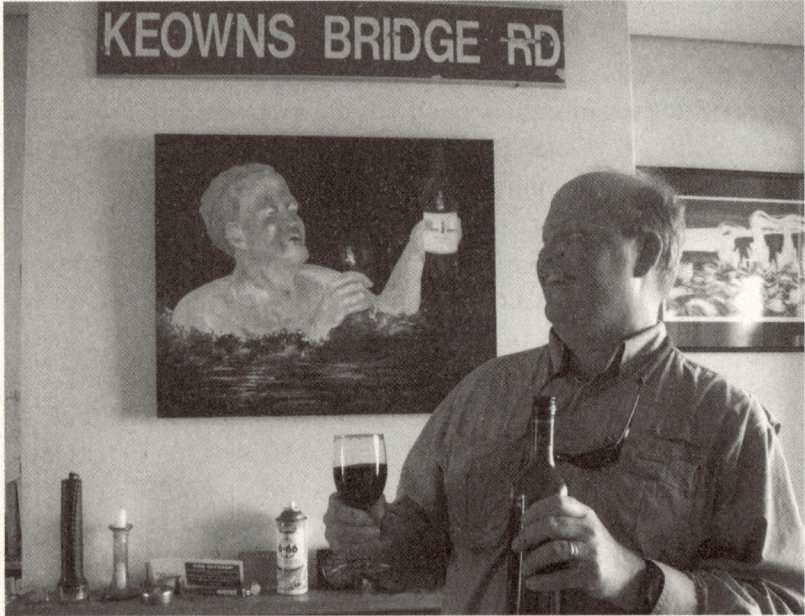
Randy at Balfour Headquarters.

below the meatball, and start a jerky retrieve. The tuna would hit and hook themselves, and if one got off there was usually another waiting to take its turn. We all landed fish, and Dougal was on his second or third, working it in, when the line went slack and in the clear water right beside the boat he saw the pale belly of a rolling shark.

We fished for a little longer, and Bubble landed one more tuna, but the sharks had taken over. They were all around the boats — bullsharks, huge brutes that homed in on each hooked fish, leaving nothing but the clean-cut head. Soon there was a swarm of them, circling and sliding up from astern and cruising alongside, watching, rolling away.

It was a slaughter, a sacrifice of tuna. We were far out to sea in a rising wind, so Fish decided to call it quits and find somewhere to put ashore and have some lunch. We found a little cove shielded from the surf and ran the boats up on the beach and lay on the sand drinking cold beer and thinking, mostly about sharks.

Two-Pies was especially vehement. One monster, he said — one evil brute — had followed his tuna right up to the boat and chopped it in two like a mackerel. Teeth the size of beer cans. It could have swallowed a pig, Two-Pies said. Those tuna are basically fucked.

But the Aussies had a different view. The tuna were faster than the sharks, they said. In the open sea they were safe, and even beneath a meatball they would normally be too agile for a shark to catch. But a hooked tuna has nowhere to go, and the sharks had worked out the connection between the sound of outboards and the presence of anglers and the near-certainty of an easy feed. Fish grinned ruefully and shrugged his shoulders. They're smart bastards, he said. There's no way round it.

For the next few days there were storms on the Gulf, huge seas breaking on the beaches. We stayed in sheltered water, fishing the mangrove inlets close to Weipa, and one morning we went across to the port, where the ore-carriers were loaded with bauxite. There was always a queue of these big, ugly ships lined up, honking their klaxons and taking their turn at the tall wharves beneath rattling conveyors of ore. It was hardly an idyllic environment, and I assumed that Fish was providing an obligatory glimpse of Weipa's industrial raison d'être. But no, we were here for the fishing.

We motored through the loose rows of tankers, tiny beneath the rusty walls, moving closer to the central wharf, and came right up to the hull of the ship that was being loaded. It was still nearly empty, its Plimsoll line far out of the water and its exposed plates draped with goose barnacles and algae. The ore thumped inside, shivering the water, and Fish stopped the boat and gave Kevin a rod and put him on the casting deck. Hit the ship, he said. Just cast straight at the hull and let it sink.

Kevin was an accomplished operator by now. He worked the line out and shot the looped coils and the lure smacked against the wall of the tanker. It dropped back into the water, and Kevin waited, professionally poised. The lure sank for about seven seconds and something seized it and went for the bottom. Kevin's poise was history. The rod bent over and Kevin stepped back, skidding sideways on the wet deck, legs flying, the reel spinning, the butt of the rod jammed into his crotch and the tip scraping against the bow. He was gone for sure, I thought, but Fish grabbed him just in time. The line kept going out.

Kevin's luck held, as always. He got back to his feet as the fish reached the seabed and stopped. He recovered some line, gradually winning against a succession of high-speed plunges. He pumped and wound for some minutes, slowly regaining his composure. He got the fish up, splashing beside the boat, but it took off again at the first touch of the net, as fast as ever, straight down.

An audience of Chinese sailors had appeared, right above us on the rail of the ship, cheering and laughing at Kevin's antics. He paid no heed. He was talking to the fish, cursing and cajoling, working the reel until eventually he got it alongside again — and again it disappeared. But the third time he held on tight and rolled it into the net. It was a fifteen-pound golden trevally, the first I had seen, a gorgeous bully of a fish, a machine of muscle

Bubble and tuna.

and metal. Fish took a photo and lowered it carefully back and the Chinese howled in dismay.

It was a bizarre kind of angling, our three little boats lined up under the kelp-hung cliff of the carrier. The water was clear, but the fish were hidden beneath the ship, visible only when they shot out to take a lure. Fish reckoned they lived there permanently, shifting casually from ship to ship, sitting upside down among the weeds of consecutive hulls, the resident population of a transient, inverted seabed, but I'm sure this was just a story for the punters.

Permanent or not, there were plenty of trevally, and several times we had three going at once, the lines crossing and tangling between the boats and the fish sunk far below in an orange ball of confusion. They were all between fifteen and twenty pounds, mighty in the power of their first mad run, and Kevin caught nine in the end — more than anybody else.

There was a big party that night with Fish and the other guides. It was a great Australian party on a deck at the beach with beer and champagne and seafood and a hot pool that Bubble wound up in, drunk with a couple of girls. People sat up to their necks in the pool and smoked and flicked ash and swapped stories, sometimes about the fishing. The guides were curious about New Zealand, and especially about our fascination with rivers and trout, which to an angler in Queensland made no sense. How could such a small and colourless creature be worthy of such enthusiasm? We of course waxed eloquent on the sterling qualities of *Salmo trutta*: its legendary guile, its superior intelligence, its refined and classical beauty. It was not the size or the power of the fish, we explained. It was the subtlety of the pursuit, and the intimate beauty of where trout lived. All fishing was good, of course, and Weipa was wonderful, but nothing could ever come close to the sublime addiction of fishing for trout in rivers. That was our story, anyway.

On the final day of the trip I was scheduled to fish with Two-Pies. We got up at dawn, as usual, and drove to the harbour with Notso, the youngest of the guides. The stormy weather was gone and we motored behind the other two boats, dancing lightly on criss-crossing wakes across the calm surface of the bay. We were bound for the ocean, or so I thought, but then Notso peeled off and headed for the nearby shoreline. He crept along the shallows close to the mangroves, and then suddenly accelerated hard into a wide, shallow opening that led through the mangroves and into a hidden lagoon. The land all around this sheltered water was flat and scrubby, with tall bush further back, and the lagoon itself was full of dead trees, protruding from the surface and embedded in the muddy shore.

Notso idled between the snags, following a channel that led into a narrowing bay. On either side were mudflats, chocolate-coloured, exposed by the tide, and as the channel tightened the current increased. We were in the mouth of a little river.

It was still quite early, the sun just over the trees and a slight mist still on the water. Notso tied up to a dead tree in the centre of the stream and we started casting, one at each end of the boat. We caught fish almost immediately — small queenfish — and we had to kill a couple that were bleeding from damage to the gills. No good, said Notso, so we reeled in and moved on, disturbing a very big crocodile that was sunning itself on a mudbank. It slithered and half-ran into the water and disappeared with a great splash and Two-Pies looked pleased, announcing that it was definitely a man-eater. Then a sea eagle flew over, about fifty feet up, the shadow of its wings like a blanket across the boat.

Notso stood up. He killed the motor and picked up one of the queenfish and held it above his head. He moved the dead fish in a slow arc and the eagle turned its head and looked down. He tossed the fish into the water, and the eagle banked like a Stuka. It came straight towards us, the wind whistling in its feathers. It struck the water at the side of the boat, talons first, wings outstretched, magnificent. It laboured up in a fountain of spray, pumping the air, the queenfish dangling, and flew to the top branch of a big leafless tree. Notso smiled like a showman.

We continued upstream a long way. The river became shallower, with large boulders in the bed, until there was barely enough draught for the boat in the faster places, and Notso got out and pushed. The air was warming in the rising sun, and the bush was coming to life. Rosellas, hundreds at a time, flew up and down at treetop height, raising an amazing racket, while beneath them, just above our heads, whizzed families of ducks, and the river-bank trees were filled with tiny iridescent birds the size of sparrows.

We stopped and fished in a few places, without result. It was difficult to imagine what our quarry might be, so far from the sea and in such confined surroundings, but Notso seemed unperturbed. He seemed to think that, as river-besotted New Zealanders, we would appreciate this Queensland equivalent of our favourite native habitat. He identified each new kind of bird, handing us the binoculars and passing out cans of beer. Birds, he said, were more interesting than fish. They were far more highly evolved, and light years ahead of fish in terms of intelligence and complexity of behaviour. Which was right, of course; but we were here to fish, and there were no fish. It was like a dud day on the Mataura, apart from the crocodiles, and Two-Pies was getting scratchy.

The channel became wider and deeper, more like a canal than a river, with clay banks and no perceptible current. It was close to midday, and the wind from the Gulf was bending the tops of the trees, carrying with it the dim boom of surf on a distant beach. But down in our sheltered green alley there was perfect calm, the surface untroubled, the boat nosing quietly among beds of lilies that grew out from the banks and sometimes met in the middle.

Notso anchored in a long, wide pool with flowering bushes overhanging the water, and Two-Pies and I stood at the ends of the boat and cast towards the opposing fringes of the lilies. It was thirsty work. The sun was directly overhead, and there were still no fish, so we knocked off for another beer. It was lunchtime anyway so the beer was followed by chilled wine and a picnic of salad and salami, smoked chicken, cheese and bread.

The boat swayed gently on the end of its rope, and the wine — a Kiwi sauvignon blanc — induced a pleasant paralysis. There was no sound but the lapping of water. Nothing stirred, not even the birds, and in our happy lassitude the effort of fishing no longer seemed very important. Two-Pies swigged and made no complaint. One more bottle, I thought. A few more glasses and then a snooze.

I awoke to shouting. Notso and Two-Pies had disappeared. We were still anchored in the same place, although the air seemed cooler and the sun had fallen towards the treetops. There were more yelps and a series of splashes, and I got up and looked over the console. Two-Pies and Notso were on the front deck and Two-Pies was connected to a fast-moving fish. It jumped again, shoulder-high, curved in a half-circle like a salmon. Two-Pies let out another yip, but the line went slack. Bad luck, said Notso.

I went to the stern of the boat and started casting with the same lure I was using earlier. Nothing happened for three or four retrieves, but on the next one there was a flurry among the lilies and a puff of silt and a fish emerged, heading straight for my lure. It stopped, and then it came on, in little, darting advances. When it reached the lure I tightened but it wasn't hooked. Not so fast, said Notso. Wait till they close their mouths.

Two-Pies had got another one, and it was dancing all over the river. It went from one side to the other, and under the boat and out again, all the while leaping like a rainbow. It was only a small fish by Australian standards — about four pounds — but supple and wild as a weasel. It did everything a trout would do attempting to escape, leaping high, working the snags, diving into the weed. I put another cast close to the lilies and there was an immediate eruption and a mushroom of silt and a fish shot out, and this time I waited and watched and when its mouth closed on the lure I was in business.

They were barramundi, and there was a whole school of them hiding in the lilies. They had no fear in approaching the lure, but were tricky to hook, and so powerful that we lost quite a few that got under the snags. One of them, played-out and almost at the

Sharked.

side of the boat, was bitten in half by an unseen shark, reminding me I was still in Australia. We caught thirty-six in just over an hour, all close to the same size, and then, as abruptly as it had begun, it was over.

We motored back downstream in the soft evening air, drinking the last of the beer. The tide was coming in, filling the channel and flooding the mudbanks, and the river was now easily negotiable. Notso was pleased with his day. His gamble had worked, and he explained about the barramundi. They were a peculiar kind of fish, he said. The ones we were catching were all males. They lived in the rivers for two or three years, and then they changed into females and shifted down to the sea. A mature female could be as big as a hundred pounds — and then they were dynamite. Then they were really worth catching.

It was almost dark in the bush when we reached the lagoon, and Notso drove cautiously till he found the gap in the mangroves and powered through to the still-bright waters of the Gulf. The sun wallowed on a hazy horizon, and the wind had abated to a cool ocean breeze. In twenty minutes we would be back in Weipa, drinking beer and yarning with the boys.

That was magic, said Two-pies. Pure bloody magic.

The barramundi, do you mean? Notso's face was mischievous in the orange light.

Two-Pies laughed. Oh alright, Notso, he said. Not just the barramundi. Everything. The fish and the birds and the sea and the crocs — the whole thing has been amazing. The big fish, too; but those little buggers in the lily beds — now they were really something. Just sitting in the weeds, they were, letting us cast for half the day, ignoring us, doing nothing. And then all of a sudden they all come out, like trout at the start of a hatch.

Notso grinned. The subtlety of the chase, he said. The cunning of the prey. The classic perfection of the four-pound barra . . .

Two-Pies punched him in the shoulder. That's right, he said. Four pounds is exactly right. We're fly-fishing, don't you remember? And as soon as I get home I'll send you some flies. Dry flies, Notso — you never can tell.

That was the end of our time in Weipa. The next morning we flew back across the strange, smoking land, and down the endless coast and over the sea to New Zealand. Back to green fields and rain, and cool rivers, and away from the wonders of Australia.

N

Thomas River
Haast
Haast River
Hunter River
Cascade River
Cameron Creek
Young River
Big Bay
Makarora River
Dingle Burn
Pyke River
Hollyford River
Ahuriri River

Omarama

Milford Sound

Wanaka

Queenstown
Cromwell
85

Alexandra
8

Te Anau

Nokomai

Manapouri
6

Lumsden
Ardlussa
Balfour HQ
Mandeville
90
8

Gore
1
1

Grebe River
Borland Burn
Aparima River
Oreti River
Invercargill
96
6
1

Balclutha

Clutha River
Pomahaka River
Waikaia River
Waimea Stream
Mataura River

94
99

0   50 km

The best pool on the Dingle.

Dougal, Turner and Two-Pies — about to
cross the Haast River on a raft.

Turner. Fiordland boating days.

There was an endless supply of venison.

Carol regains her nerve.

Carol in the Dingle.

Crossing the Alps in the S7.

A beauty from the Aparima.

A tussock.

Kevin nails the dinner.

Morsie at Nokomai.

Summer in the Waikaia.

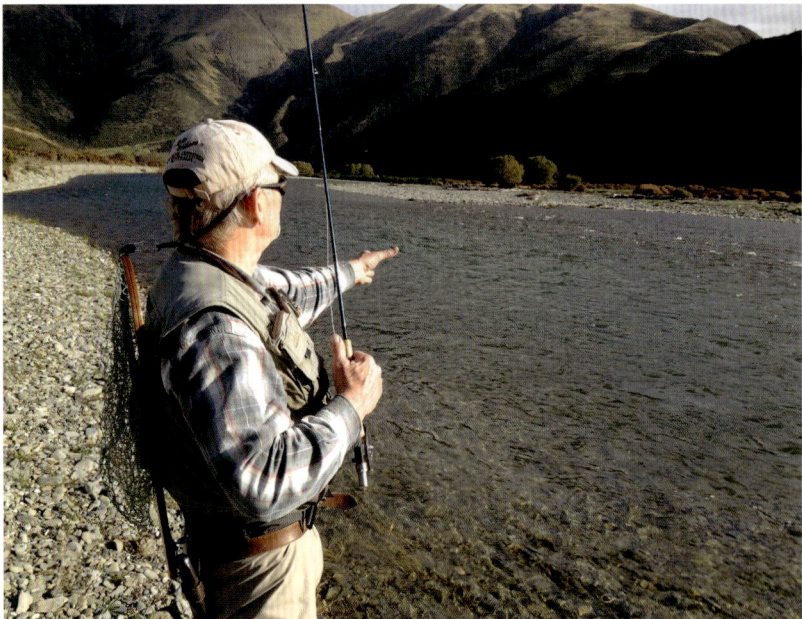

A no-fail ripple on the Mataura.

SEVEN

Your Place or Mine

'Everyone should possess a river,'
wrote Ben Hur Lampman, long ago.
'Everyone should own a river, to have
and to hold for his own. And there
is this about a river, that a thousand
may have such rights in its glancing
brightness, the moody green secrecy
of its eddies, as one possesses.'

I have been lucky then, in my lifetime, to have owned my share
of rivers 'by natural right', as Lampman termed it. I have
owned them, not through title and exclusive seizure, but in
the only way that anyone can ever really own anything on this
ephemeral planet: by familiarity, exposure, knowledge stored up
over years.

My first New Zealand river was in the Bay of Plenty: the blue-
skied, bright-watered Wheao. There were numerous contenders
— the Whirinaki, the Rangitaiki, the Waioeka — but the Wheao
was a dream of perfection come true. I can see it still in reverie
with an effortless, startling clarity: its swift, unvarying flow, its
jungle banks, and its powerful, beautiful trout.

The Wheao never flooded (or at least not in my memory). Its pumice soil was a mighty sponge, and weeks of rain leaked only enough to shorten the flax and faintly haze the water. And the wind was no more than a gentle breeze, no matter what the weather. Day after day in the yellow heat of summertime, with the white clouds flying in a tumult aloft, and the pines swaying on their pumice bluffs, the Wheao ran inviolate. I never saw another angler.

But my ownership of the Wheao was to last for only two seasons — scarcely enough, indeed, to claim any natural right of possession — though I fished there with an addict's devotion on every chance I got. Then the hydro-vandals destroyed it, a crime that grieves me still.

The South Island then was just names on a map: the innumerable names of rivers. And the West Coast was an unexplored wilderness where even the locals scarcely knew the waters they owned and the wealth of trout contained in them. I roamed the roads and fished at random, stopping at what rivers I came to. Once, on the highway bridge at Jacks Stream, I saw an enormous trout rising, directly beneath the bridge. I can scarcely believe this image now, for such a fish in such a place would be impossible in today's high-pressured streams. But there it was, and I raised it easily in a couple of casts, and landed it, and let it go, a black-and-silver torpedo so unusually marked that I never knew if it was a rainbow or a brown.

And then, the last, and wildest place — Fiordland — with rivers too many to count. I camped and tramped, and fell in love with the Worsley, visiting it season by season in triumph and disaster. Bliss, the stuff of an angling delirium — or weeks of rain in the Henderson Hut while the mountains dissolved and disappeared and a family of accusing weka stood sodden on the porch.

For several years I seemed to enjoy an exclusive lease on the Borland Burn. There was never another angler, never footprints in the mud or sand, yet an all-weather road led almost to the river bank, and I knew there must be others. I was lucky then, as were these unseen fellow anglers — for we never met, and, however many of us there were, the stream was virgin, new-made on every visit, glittering with wild promise. I caught a trout, my biggest ever on the Borland, one summer day when the beech-mast was thick and the forest alive with mice. It was an eight-pounder, dramatically painted, with eight tiny mice in its belly.

The world is more crowded now, and ownership of a river is not what it used to be. A condominium, or an apartment, not a country estate, is all that most of us may hope for, and the thousand tenants that Lampman referred to have become, even in remote New Zealand, our everyday reality.

My holding now is the Mataura. Not all of it, for I've never been keen on the high-density reaches downstream of Gore. But from Mandeville to Nokomai I search the ever-changing banks of the upper river, season after season. No gravel-bed shifts but I am aware of it; no ripple erodes, or expands, but I take note, and the yearly echelons of lovely trout, as many or as few as the give and take of the river dictates, are as distinct in my mind as separate vintages.

On the last day of last season, with the willows still green and the mayfly nymphs still submerged in the confusion of a warm autumn, the Mataura was acting fishless. Nothing moved but the water, and the single trout I had managed to raise had mischievously avoided hooking. It was late, the sun low against the darkening hills, and the silver surface inscrutable. But the ripple before me had never failed.

A trial cast or two in the barren tail, then up to where the trout would be, line diagonal and mended intently. A pause, an instinctive strike, and a fish was on — turning, rolling, and powering downstream for the inevitable maze of willows. It was the old choice: lean on the trout, and break it, or allow it into sanctuary. I leant, and the leader parted.

Seasons should never end like this: wonderful seasons especially. I caught the trailing nylon out of the air, and found both nymphs had gone — not just the point fly, as I had expected. The break was at a bloodknot, far up. I would have to rebuild the leader.

Five knots, threaded against the fading light, and I returned

No willows. An easy ripple on
the Mataura at Nokomai.

to the knee-deep water, tossing an identical duo of nymphs into the shadows of the same location. Everything seemed replicated. The line stopped on cue, scarcely visible, and the fish took off on its ordained trajectory. But this time I was fearful of a break, and the trout got into the willows.

There was no chance. A few head-shakings among the sunken roots and the line went dead. Four flies gone in a couple of casts, and not a fish to show for them. I reeled mechanically, all my great days forgotten in the moment's desolation. But what was this? There were flies still there, in a tangle.

The knots were intact, and my two nymphs were still attached — with, seen against the dimming skylight, two more flies: the previous pair, beadhead hooked to beadhead. I picked them apart, wondering, and saw glinting on the point of one hook a single scale, translucent.

Seasons cannot really end like this, with the ghost of a trout in the dying day. I went back to the water, now velvety-black, and covered the remainder of the ripple. A little trout flashed up, and was hooked, and soon lay on the stones, as fat as a grub. To my gourmet eyes he was perfect.

Everyone should possess a river, for strange things happen on rivers if you own them, and know them well, and care for them enough. Things that by rights and on ordinary days ought to be impossible.

EIGHT

Ethics Afield

Albert was upset. His face was grim. He gazed at the ceiling and sighed forlornly and drained the last of his gin. The bloody fly was stuck in my earlobe, he said. It was a Hare and Copper, size ten, wrapped in lead. And this disgusting clown — from Auckland, I think he said he was — this foul fellow waded right across in front of me and asked could he have it back.

Fegelmeyer uncorked the bottle. He topped up the tumblers, saying nothing, and Albert was encouraged to continue.

These people are savages, he said. No standards at all. Last duck-hunting season was the worst yet: an impossible, an extraordinary situation. I mean to say, how on earth does one manage an appropriate response?

To a fly in the earlobe, said Fegelmeyer.

No, no, not that. That was back in December. This was on Opening morning. I'll never forget it: a hole in the wall of the maimai, straight through at head-height. I was absent, most fortunately. I was urinating in the flax at the time, or I wouldn't be here to recall it. But what do you imagine I should have said — or done? I mean, the wretch was standing there right in front of me, smoking a fag, grinning from ear to ear.

Albert is becoming a dinosaur, like a good many of his generation. He was brought up in a different era, when sportsmanship was taken for granted, when people learned what to do by observing the behaviour of their seniors. He doesn't realise that those days have gone, and he seems to think that the degeneracy so prevalent today is some kind of temporary aberration that might be put right by a dose of friendly advice.

But people are not civilised that easily. They have to be persuaded, educated, or, in recalcitrant cases, bludgeoned into behaving decently. There is nothing at all surprising or novel about this, and it applies to everyone, including dogs and horses. The rules may change from time to time, but whatever the consensus happens to be, it has to be instilled, somehow or other, into each generation.

A written code of conduct might be helpful — assuming, of course, that those concerned are able to read — but the really strange thing is that, while there are books about everything even remotely connected with hunting and fishing, there is nothing — not even a pamphlet — on sporting ethics.

This, at first glance, is quite baffling. Why, in the prodigious annals of rod and gun, has such an essential topic been so completely neglected? There are thousands of books, spanning hundreds of years — an incomparable accumulated literature — yet hardly a mention of the time-honoured rules that, until very recent times, have made the outdoor sportsman an exemplar of civilised conduct. There are manuscripts upon the utmost trivia, whole libraries of exquisite digression, yet nothing to assist in the resolution of the situations and embarrassments that Albert now finds so disturbing.

But in truth the explanation is simple. There was no need, until now, for such a book, because it has only been in recent times that every Tom, Dick and Harriet has been let loose with a twelve-bore, or whatever. The old sporting traditions have been overthrown, trampled by the herd, and now, alas, it is too late to benignly restore them. Sterner methods will have to be employed.

Cast your mind back, if you are old enough, to the way things used to be. Picture those days and years on the stream or the marsh when persons encountered knew what was what, and could be depended upon to behave properly. Fellow shooters, for example, were well apprised of the particularities of life, and were not, upon the merest glimpse of feather or fur, liable to cut loose in mid-hello with an impromptu blast between one's knees, or past one's astonished earhole. Yet such occurrences are now commonplace.

Guns, obviously, have always had an appeal beyond their sporting or martial attributes. There have been ill-bred opportunists since the earliest times — since the flintlock, or even the firelock. But it must be said that even the lousiest Renaissance highwayman was apt to preserve a sense of occasion — of drama, even — far removed from the uncouth antics observed today.

The fate of angling was perhaps less foreordained. The long rod is a weapon of some subtlety, not readily adapted to illicit purposes, and while there have always been poachers of salmon and trout, their methods were traditionally the net and the gaff — repellent, no doubt, but at least clearly defining the calibre of those who would stoop to use them. (A distinction that has for all practical purposes vanished now, since the invention of such vulgar implements as the spinning rod and the fixed spool reel.)

Attitudes are as crucial as equipment. Where, nowadays, do we find mutual respect and empathy? Time was, as I recall, when the privacy of one's presence upon the streamside was sacrosanct, and the thought of intrusion upon what is, at best, a solitary and contemplative pursuit was not to be entertained. Field-glasses were often employed for this very purpose, and used from afar to determine the magnitude of berth necessary to obviate the possibility of a chance meeting. Thus informed, to fish within a mile of elderly, decrepit types was considered taboo, while active, mobile personages were best distanced by half a day's walk at a minimum.

All gone. All ancient history. The boors have taken over, and pristine mornings by the beckoning river, the dawn forest misty and the dew untrodden, will nowadays, more likely than not, provoke the arrival of some drooling lunatic with flippers, mask and speargun, or suchlike depraved technology.

Worst of all, by far, are the imposters who imagine they have acquired the rudiments of casting a fly. This was once an infallible criterion, and the mere possession of a fly-rod was a token, a talisman, a sure guarantee that its bearer could be trusted in the uttermost extremity. But sadly, not any longer. The last bastions of decency have crumbled, and sooner or later (if not already) the lives of all of us are doomed to be disrupted by the rude intrusion of one of these parvenu monsters. It is inevitable. It is bound to happen, and all one can do is be prepared.

They are most active at dusk, at the hour of the evening rise. Emerging then like predatory wraiths, these so-called 'anglers' appear upon the river, advancing crabwise along the banks in an absurd pretence of examining the water. Trout may well be rising, but it is no matter — they will go unnoticed by these neanderthals, who, knowing nothing of angling, must impose themselves on those who do.

You yourself, naturally, will have already marked the best fish in your favourite reach, and be patiently awaiting that precise moment in mid-hatch when the caution of the trout gives way to abandon, and even the wiliest of the wily may be seduced.

Without warning it happens. A figure scurries from the scrub behind you, and a rod-bearing wrist sails past your ear, and before you know it the interloper — to all appearances as if you do not exist — is capering beside you like a dervish. It is a provocation beyond all bearing — and entirely futile, of course, for there is not the least chance that this termite will ever catch anything. Yet there he is, arms going, line flying, snagging the foliage in front and behind and transforming the peaceful surface of your pool into a whiplashed arc of sterility.

It is over. The serenity of your evening is beyond recall, and within a few nightmare moments every trout in the vicinity has been put down for a week at least.

Be firm. There is no use in temporising in such cases; one's duty is plain. Unlimber your concealed four-ten and cock it, and administer carefully at minimum range a searing ration of number fives midway between the yokel's eyeballs. Have no qualms about the propriety of this. Tradition and justice demand it.

NINE

Albert

Albert is gone now, and his like I shall never know again. Soldier, idler, peerless sportsman, he seemed to me indestructible, his spare, powerful frame unbowed, even into his eighties.

W e were allies in spirit, despite the difference in our ages, adventuring together in those wonderful years when the war still lived in memory, and the sunny uplands of the promised future were a vision still believed.

I was teaching in Dunedin when our paths first crossed. It was a job I detested, but couldn't think how to escape. I had an old wooden villa and a neat vegetable garden and a stamp collection, and most of the people I knew were just the same: they painted their houses every few years and had a garden and a hobby and maybe a wife. It was a way of keeping sane, except in my case it wasn't working.

On Friday night I would go to the pub with the other blokes and we'd write off a few more brain cells — even though some of us had barely a quorum to start with. It was supposed to be enjoyable, and the worse you felt on Saturday morning the better it must have been on the previous evening.

Anyway, that was Fridays. The rest of the time I was sober and responsible, and so were most of my mates. We used to talk about it — responsibility. Apparently it was the thing to have.

My stamp collection was coming along nicely. I had all the aunts and uncles saving them for me, as well as one of the pretty typists in the school office, who had a brother in Tannu Tuva. His letters to her had big triangular stamps — very hard to get in the normal way of things — and they made great opportunities for flirtation. The other blokes used to be envious of me, engrossed in philatelical banter with one sweet young thing or the other. Meanwhile I was going out of my mind.

It was slightly better in the summer, when the school shut down and the kids buggered off. Several of the teachers had holiday places out at Waihola, and I bought one too, and for a fortnight or so every year we'd lie in the sun, if any, and then come back to town and dig our gardens and carry on with painting our houses. One of the blokes knew somebody in the paint business and could get it cheap, but only in one colour: lime-green. You could drive around Dunedin and pick out everybody that worked at our school from the colour of their house.

I was well on my way to the nuthouse when Albert, by some brilliant fluke of fate, dropped into my life. His truck had broken down at Waihola while we were on our New Year break, and I towed him to the garage and put him up in my spare room. We sat up all night, yarning about one thing and another, and in the spangled craziness of Albert's conversation I began to see possibilities undreamt of in the land of triangular stamps and green paint and responsibility.

Albert invited me down to his place near Gore. Forget about the garden, he said — do you know anything about fishing? I said that I did, a little bit. That I had been pretty keen when I was younger, but had given it up when I got a full-time job — a response that amused Albert no end.

Alright, he said. I'll see you in Gore on Friday.

That was the end of the teaching.

Albert introduced me to his pals — fanatics, the lot. We went fishing for trout and groper and cod all summer long. We dived for crayfish and paua, and prospected for gold to pay the bills, and went over to Stewart Island in Albert's boat and trapped possums during the winter. You didn't need a regular job, Albert explained. You could make enough money doing exactly what you liked. And in those days he was right.

Albert was the opposite of normal. He had no use for the usual conventions, and he regarded the law as a smorgasbord of voluntary options to be accepted or ignored as he pleased. He was a throwback to some earlier, more expansive era, let loose in a constipated century. He was anarchic and irrepressible, a gentleman and a misfit, and his operating principle was excess.

There was a mystery to Albert, for all that. We would go to the pub on Fridays, as everyone then did, and drink cheap beer out of two-pint jugs. Wine had not been discovered yet, or at least not in Southland, and when we were full of beer we would move on to whisky or rum. There was no café culture in those days, and pubs, it was generally understood, were places designed for getting drunk in.

It was primitive and often boisterous. Albert would sit at the table drinking round for round, laughing at the absurdities of the conversation and delivering cockeyed opinions on everything under the sun. He had a fund of stories — beguiling amalgams of fact and fiction that grew more crazily improbable as the night wore on. Believe whatever you like, he said. It doesn't make any difference.

There were always girls in the pub when Albert was there. He was a handsome man, and he treated women with an easy courtesy that never seemed to fail. He had many opportunities, and a liaison or two, but he evaded any long-term commitment. There was too much to do, he said. Too many places we still haven't seen. And anyway, there are enough married people in the world.

Albert in the Takitimus.

You could make enough money doing
exactly what you liked.

Many years afterwards, tucked among the yellowing pages of angling nostalgia and poetry and old newspaper clippings among the books and papers that Albert had left me I found a few paragraphs in his own hand.

The pleasures of life seemed simple when I was young in Tuatapere. There were pretty girls, and I had not yet discovered fishing and the riddles of the universe.

I was happy, in my way, but my innocence was to end with the beginning of the war.

I enlisted, of course, anticipating overseas adventures, but was persuaded otherwise by the SIS, and spent the duration with the commandos, training in the Takitimus. (And perhaps one day that story, too, will be told.)

I operated alone for long weeks and months, and among the skills imperative to survival in that rugged theatre, the ability to live off the land was paramount. Many was the time when in a tight spot my prowess with the Lee-Enfield ensured venison for supper. And in the hidden headwaters of the Aparima I learned the secrets of the trout, and the subtle pleasures of fishing with flies.

The war ended, and I returned to Tuatapere, and settled into my old ways again. And there I met Gladys. She was young and beautiful as the morning. We courted and made our plans — and then she told me that I must choose between love and fishing.

I was desolate, unable to react, unable

to decide. For several days I wrestled with my desires and my nature, but to no avail.

At last I knew what I must do. I would return to the lonely Takitimus, and there, in the wild fastness, I would compose myself and make my decision.

And that is what I did. Again I fished the rivers of my former delight, soothed my spirit with the sound of water flowing, rose in the dawn with the mountain mist and hunted the brown trout.

The living air cleared my mind and at length I could see my situation as though from a remote, impersonal ground. The elements of my dilemma, I now understood, were timeless: the yearning of man for freedom, and his irreconcilable need for security and bondage.

So I decided I would marry. I returned to Tuatapere, light of heart and all doubts resolved, and sought Gladys.

But she was gone.

Gone. Had the strain of waiting overcome her? Had she too been riven by some deep and unspoken anguish?

No, she had not. It was far worse than that. She had run off with a friend of mine — a worm-fisherman from Bluecliffs.

There is no honour among worm-fishermen.

TEN

Elmo

Angling is not an unduly social pursuit, but you do meet some peculiar people. Take Elmo, for example — or Colonel Guttshot, as he calls himself. I've known him for ages, ever since he came over from Texas, and most of the time we get on alright.

He's a pretty good fisherman, but he's an ex-artilleryman and an academic to boot. God knows how he found the time to do all this, but he has half a dozen degrees — most of them in economics, with one in biology as well. Some of his ideas seem sound enough, but then, every now and again, he comes out with something that makes you wonder.

His latest brainstorm was prompted by the fact that milk now costs more than beer. Most people don't find this very remarkable, but Elmo says it is. Nothing like it, apparently, has ever happened before in the entire history of humanity.

The big difference between milk and beer — so Elmo says — is that milk is an essential food, while beer is not. Beer may be a desirable commodity — one of those substances that actually make life worth living — but milk is basic nutrition, and Elmo has written a paper about it, called 'The Beer–Milk Singularity', which is causing hot debate in economic circles. I'm not up with the more technical aspects of the thing, but as a rough approximation it would seem that, historically, we have passed a significant watershed — the point where established values are inverted, where luxuries become cheaper than essentials. We have reached what the economists call a tipping-point, and unfortunately there is no way back.

Elmo is retired now, and lives not far down the road from me, at Mandeville. He has a house beside the airfield, about a quarter of a mile from the river, and we had arranged to go fishing together on the last day of the season. I got another speeding ticket and arrived late, and he was working through a big, deep ripple just above the township when I finally caught up with him. He seemed in a remarkably cheerful mood, although he had been there all morning and was still to catch a fish. He was philosophic about his latest ideas. Every cloud has its silver lining, he believes, and so it shall be with the Beer–Milk tipping-point, despite its far-reaching implications. Tipping-points are nothing new, he assures me. They happen all the time. But the interesting thing, according to Elmo, is that we now have a plague of them, all occurring simultaneously. There is this business of the planet heating up, and the ice caps melting, and Tuvalu going underwater. There's species extinction, and gay marriage, peak oil, dry rivers, dead oceans, you name it. There's a whole heap of potential tipping-points, and all of them, Elmo says, are closely interrelated. They're all a consequence of the runaway biological success of our own species, *Homo sapiens.*

This might appear alarming, or possibly even terminal, but Elmo seems quite relaxed. There is too much gloom in the world,

Elmo, aka Colonel Guttshot.

he thinks. People become all worked up about trifles: even worse, about absolute inevitabilities such as the end of life as we know it.

Life as we know it has always been ending, Elmo says, and to imagine otherwise is to ignore the transparent fact that human history is nothing but the sorry record of how we bugger things up, and the only surprising thing about it is that people keep getting upset. Think back as far as you like, and it's still the same — Stone Agers, for example, going out of business when somebody invented bronze. Arabs and Africans, fighting with spears, being slaughtered wholesale by a few dozen white blokes with machine guns. Tipping-points, you see. Something new comes along and it's goodbye to what you thought was your civilisation.

Elmo's head is stuffed with obscure and ostensibly unrelated facts. He cobbles them together and spills them out, and the result is often impressive. But there was something far too breezy and convenient about this cartoon summation of all of human history. How, I wanted to know, did events in the Stone Age relate to our present predicaments?

Alright, he said. Look at it this way. It's all to do with how things change. It used to be slow, but now it's going faster and faster. Twenty years — only a heartbeat in historical time — and all our old assumptions have been turned inside out. The university, for example: one of the most ancient of our institutions, bigger than ever — but for the first time in a thousand years the average graduate doesn't read and can hardly write. And look at what's happened to the cost of things. Cars used to be expensive and petrol was cheap. Now it's the other way round. Phone calls likewise: used to be prohibitive, now cost bugger-all. The rivers — this river and all the rest of them. Do you remember, not so long ago, when we had them more or less to ourselves, before the big, cheap jets from Australia? The good old days, remember them? And there's didymo, of course; and the bag limits keep going down. And just about everything has become dirt cheap: TVs, power tools, whisky, fancy fly-rods, you name it.

All of this, according to Elmo, is the inevitable consequence of progress. We no longer need workers, so we pay them the dole or park them in the so-called universities. We have finally solved the age-old problem of production. Consumer goods spew out of the factories, untouched by human hand, priced at next to nothing. It was the dream of mankind for centuries.

Elmo was tottering around in a powerful current near midstream, his line snagged on the opposite bank. He can be an entertaining old bastard, but this spiel, I thought, was pushing things a bit too far. What's wrong with cars that people can afford? I wanted to know. Or TVs, or fishing tackle, or warehouses full of whisky? What's wrong with any of it? OK, there are a few problems, but I don't see you growing your own spuds and fishing with braided horsehair.

Nothing wrong, said Elmo, breaking off his fly and winding the line in. Nothing wrong at all. In fact, I entirely agree with you: our material blessings are not at all to be disparaged. But you're missing the point. The difficulty is that not everything is getting cheaper.

Like what?

Food. Haven't you noticed? Food gets dearer all the time. It's a worldwide trend, and it's going to get worse, because, worldwide, there are too many customers and not enough grub. And TVs are no compensation. You can't eat a TV, at any price, or a fridge, or a boron bloody fly-rod. And you only need a new one every ten years or so. But you need food every day. When a CD player costs less than a kilo of cod you have to admit we've got things ass-about-face.

Elmo has recently resigned from his job as head of the Tomagalak Thinktank. The thinktank's essential work is done, he says, and there is no good reason to continue. He intends to go fishing, full-time, with a spot of gardening when the trout aren't rising. It is a selfish decision, he freely admits, but then as he points out, almost everyone is selfish. It's our single defining characteristic. It has got us to where we are now, masters of the planet, arbiters of the fate of the Earth, or, as the doomsters say, up the creek without a paddle.

The low overcast had turned into rain, and I decided not to

argue any more, or we'd be stuck out here all day. But Elmo kept talking, wobbling around on the slippery bottom and expanding on his view of the facts. Which, all up, are pretty dismal. We're on the edge of a cliff, he says — or, to be more accurate, quite a number of cliffs — and there's nothing to be done about it. The economy — the whole global event — is floating along in a deluge of cooked-up money. It's a magnificent, inglorious Ponzi scheme, and the bankers and their pals are covering it up while they loot what's left of the till. The bust-up is inevitable — and, Elmo thinks, the sooner this happens the better.

The crisis is over, Elmo, I said. We're in recovery now — or hadn't you heard?

Elmo started giggling. He was still standing in the river, though he wasn't fishing, and now he was snuffling with inexplicable mirth, and I was beginning to think that his own personal tipping-point was not too far away.

Forget the recovery, he said. It's like those trillions the bankers are inventing: Monopoly money, fodder for TV-watchers. But don't worry about the bloody economy. What was it the greenies used to say: think globally, act locally? Well, try thinking about this locality. It's not too bad. We have everything we could need: enough technology to get by with and plenty of hydro-juice to drive it — and with only four million or so, we'll always have tons of food.

I thought you said that food is going to get more and more expensive?

It will, but not necessarily for us. We live in a land of plenty, and once we ditch the trade agreements food will go back to being cheap. The whole countryside is coming down with sheep and lambs and cattle-beasts, and the forests are full of deer. There are rabbits and ducks — meat galore — and fish. People are catching beautiful fish, like trout, and throwing them back in the river. Wild, fresh trout, premium tucker, totally organic — and they toss them back in the river.

I don't see you tossing too many back at the moment.

A little flight of teal skimmed past just overhead, wings

thrumming, and Elmo gazed pensively after them. He waded to the shore and tossed his rod into a gorse bush. He looked quizzically at me for a moment, and pulled two bottles of beer out of his day pack. Relax, he said. The next few years will be interesting. The only thing anyone can be sure of is that it won't be business as usual.

And you're bailing out?

Yes, said Elmo. The old rat race has had its day, and until they organise a new rat race you might as well please yourself.

He popped the cap from his bottle and raised it, grinning in mock salute. Here's to the future, he said. Happy days, and the end of life as we know it.

ELEVEN

Where to Go

Years ago, when I was young and had plenty of money, I lived for a while in the little town of Houston, in northern British Columbia, not far from the Kispiox River.

Houston was surrounded by wonderful fishing in those days, and the Kispiox, about fifty miles down the road, had recently become famous on account of the very large steelhead that spawned in it. These fish were genuine monsters, and in fact the three biggest steelhead ever caught had been taken from the Kispiox about ten years before I went to live there. Not surprisingly, therefore, on the strength of this fully verified record, the good folks of Houston had christened their town 'The Steelhead Capital of the World'.

So far, so good. Business in Houston prospered. Anglers came in their thousands — drawn by a number of glowing stories in *Field and Stream* about the magnificent steelhead of the Kispiox. Fish were caught by the truckload — steelhead, king salmon and coho, as well as the year-round resident rainbows. Lodges were built, and new roads were pushed further and further — not just into the Kispiox, but into all the other local rivers, which up until then had been hardly fished at all. This was progress: money was made, and everyone was happy. But the biggest fish had already been caught, and despite a growing army of anglers there was no improvement in the record. Some people, in fact, were rude enough to claim that the fish were getting scarcer and smaller each year, and a few — including newcomers such as I — began to wonder if Houston really was the steelhead capital of the world.

Being a trout-fishing capital, in other words, might be just a preliminary step to being an ex-trout-fishing capital — and we need to bear this in mind when we examine the competing claims of various angling locations, especially in New Zealand.

The trout-fishing capital business is not as simple as it looks. There are dozens of capitals. There are lake trout capitals and river trout capitals, and then there are separate capitals for each species of trout. A few of them may be genuine, with swags of big fish, easy to catch, even by total wombats. But such situations are exceptional, and temporary at best, and most trout-fishing capitals are old fished-out holiday hellholes, long overrun by swarms of itinerant anglers, guides, gofers, touts, bludgers, concessionaires, hoteliers, lodge owners, ladies of the night, and the employees of hydroelectric companies. None of these places will ever confess that the good old days are over and the fishing is pretty well stuffed.

This situation is confusing enough, but the expansion of the tourist racket has made it almost impossible to arrive at an objective view of the merits of any particular trout-fishing destination. Tourists, it has been discovered, are suckers for trout. It appeals to their sense of snobbery, because trout, especially if caught on a fly, are symbolic of leisure and aristocracy. Trout are game fish, not coarse fish: they are the squire's fish, not the servant's. So the promise of trout-fishing will nail the tourists every time.

There is now a well-recognised procedure to becoming a trout-fishing capital. The first and most important thing is to put up a big sign — or better still, a big fibreglass trout — at the entrance to your town. Then make a promotional video, get television and radio time, and print lots of pamphlets filled with pictures of big fish. It helps, of course, if there are trout in the vicinity, but, such is the innocence of the average tourist 'angler', this is not essential. Visitors will come and money will flow regardless. And if anybody complains about the lack of trout they can be assured that, yes, the fishing is tough right now, but 'you should have been here on Thursday'. That will pacify most of them — and anyway, you've already got the money.

There is no point in bemoaning this kind of fraudulence. It is standard practice throughout the tourist world — and a good thing too, or the tourism industry would collapse. But it does present a serious problem for the genuine non-tourist angler, who would like to do a bit of fishing in new surroundings but is wary of being conned. How, amid such reams of exaggeration and barefaced lies, does he find some honest information?

This problem is worse in New Zealand than almost anywhere else. The whole Kiwi economy relies on tourism, and the trout-fishing angle is now recognised as a sure-fire moneyspinner. Most towns promote themselves as angling destinations, and on top of that there are two officially designated 'Trout-fishing Capitals of the World': Turangi, in the North Island, and Gore, down in the South. They are both situated on rivers, and, thanks to a barrage of virtually interchangeable promotional material, it is almost impossible to choose between them.

There's no point in consulting the media, or writing to the tourist board or the local chamber of commerce. They're all in it together, and you'll simply get another parcel of pamphlets with pictures of big fish. You need first-hand information. You need the honest, unbiased opinions of people with no financial interest — real anglers like yourself.

I could, of course, provide you with my own opinion of these two so-called trout-fishing capitals. Forty years of residence on the

All you need is a big plastic trout.

banks of the Mataura would seem an adequate qualification, but alas, I have no personal experience of Turangi.

Not to worry, though, for I have located several highly respected anglers, gentlemen fly-fishers of unimpeachable integrity, who are equally familiar with both these regions. Their assessments, which follow, are untainted by any bias, personal, professional, or financial.

Two-Pies Dean is a fly-fisherman of fifty years' experience, who maintains holiday homes on the Tongariro, near Turangi, and on the Mataura, just upstream of Gore. He divides his time between them — although, he says, he probably now spends more time in the south. 'It's a nostalgia thing,' says Dean. 'I remember it thirty years ago, when the fishing around Gore was brilliant — which it still is, of course, at Turangi.'

Dean's assessment is straightforward: 'The Tongariro is un-beatable — the best trout stream in New Zealand, and almost certainly the best in the world. I never start before ten o'clock, and usually bag a limit by lunchtime. Then, after a bottle of wine and a lie-down, I knock off another limit in the evening. It doesn't really matter what fly you use — you're going to catch lots of fish.'

And what about Gore, where Dean mainly fishes the Mataura?

'Well, I put in a big effort there last season, whenever the weather allowed. The river was frozen early on, and it snowed till after Christmas. Then there were gales and about half a dozen floods, which slowed things down. But I did catch a couple of small ones near Mandeville, in February.'

'Two fish for the season. Was that the lot?'

'I got a half-pounder in the Oreti as well — that's only about an hour from Gore. It was a pretty skinny fish, though. And I hooked another one on the last day of April, in the middle of a

The Mataura. Nothing left worth catching.

blizzard. But it got off. Then I flew up to Turangi to catch a few more limits.'

As Dean says, fishing down south is a nostalgia thing for him, and he is driven by the hope that the wonderful Mataura hatches of yesteryear will come back someday. He confesses he is a bit of a masochist.

Dougal Rillstone is another lifetime fly-fisherman. Born and raised in Gore, he knows the region intimately, and confesses a parochial attachment to the Mataura that disillusionment is unlikely to extinguish. 'I grew up fishing the Mataura,' he says, 'and I suppose I always will — although it is terribly sad to see its condition now.'

The whole Gore region is in similar decline, according to Rillstone, with outbreaks of disease, pollution, and invasive algae that seem likely to kill off any remaining fish. Despite it all, however, he remains loyal to his birthplace, and still spends a lot of time on the Mataura. 'I just carry the rod out of habit these days — but really it's hardly worth it. I take the dog and we tramp for miles along the river. I do it for the exercise, mainly, and not having to stop and fish is a bonus for the dog.'

Rillstone is an ex-Oceania fly-fishing champion, and he still loves catching trout. He flies regularly to Turangi, where he hangs out at Dean's place and knocks out limit bags of big rainbows with clockwork regularity. 'The dog hates it at Turangi,' he jokes, 'because I only go to one pool in the morning, get a limit in half an hour, and never need to move.'

An obvious picture was emerging by the time I had interviewed Dean and Rillstone. But these were both Southern men, and whatever their apparent objectivity they may have been influenced, subconsciously, in favour of their native patch, so I sought further confirmation from a third source — a much-travelled international expert with no local ties or nostalgic associations.

Rick Boebel — Bubble to his friends — is an American from Louisiana, who grew up hand-wrestling giant catfish from the muddy bayous of the Mississippi. 'They ran up to about four hundred pounds,' recalls Boebel, 'but, as a sport, it was somewhat lacking in finesse, and I gave it up after a near-drowning and several amputations.' Family and work then intervened, and Boebel abandoned fishing for a decade, until, following a meteoric career in the habergropery trade, he moved to Turangi in search of 'peace, pleasure, and fly-fishing'.

Turangi, he reports, was everything he had dreamt of, and limit bags of big fish were a daily occurrence. Nevertheless, in 2001, he shifted south, and it was in his luxurious lodge in the little village of Balfour, a few miles from Gore and a stone's throw from the Mataura, that we discussed the rewards and vicissitudes of the full-time angling life.

'I didn't think I would ever leave Turangi,' said Boebel with evident emotion, 'but my health was on the point of collapse. It was the continuous idyllic weather and the volcanic air, you see. That sulphur — or whatever it is up there — was affecting my lungs, and my only chance of recovery was to go somewhere real, real cold, with constant gales for maximum wind-chill. The doctors were unanimous.'

Balfour, as Boebel discovered after months of research, fitted this description perfectly.

'It is so cold here that there is almost no humidity. Even in summertime the windows are all iced-up till lunchtime, and it blows non-stop. I'm feeling ever so much better.'

'And what about the fishing?'

'It's really good. I have a boat down at Bluff, and whenever the gales let up we scoot out and catch blue cod.'

'No — the trout-fishing, I mean. This place is supposed to be the trout-fishing capital of the world.'

Boebel looked blank for a moment, as though misunderstanding my question, and then began to laugh.

'Trout-fishing,' he chortled. 'You've come to the wrong place, buddy. There's no trout-fishing around here.'

So there it is. As I said at the start, you need to be very suspicious about the trout-fishing capital business. There's too much skull-duggery about, and too much misinformation and straight-out lies. But I think that discerning anglers will appreciate, and be grateful for, the testimony elicited from my panel of totally disinterested experts. And tourist anglers, especially, need no longer be confused by the commercial claims of New Zealand's rival angling capitals. The message is clear: if you are looking for trout stay away from Gore. There is no point at all in going to Gore, or anywhere near the Mataura River. Go to Turangi every time — the one and only — the Trout-fishing Capital of the World!

TWELVE

Wordplay

Angling is often described as a 'sport' —
a broad classification that includes such
things as rugby, cricket, lawn bowls,
ice hockey, quoits, boxing and skittles.
There are few common denominators,
if any, between angling and any of these
pastimes, which, even more confusingly,
are commonly referred to as games.

Games themselves ramify in endless directions — to
tiddlywinks, Scrabble, Monopoly, poker, or any of the
other amusements that people have invented to pass the
time. And all of these widely differing activities are subsumed
in the blanket term 'recreation', which, of course, is so baggy a
usage as to be no use at all. Collecting beer mats is a recreation,
and so is jumping off high buildings with a parachute.

If angling is a sport it is of a special kind. It evolved through
many centuries, with its origins in a time when obtaining enough
food to stay alive took precedence over recreation. It was just one
of a group of related outdoor pursuits that included falconry, fox-
hunting, stag-coursing and wildfowling, whose traditions go back

to our agrarian past, and to our ancestry as hunter-gatherers. These activities, which until very recently did form a coherent category, were originally known as 'field sports' — or, more accurately, as 'blood sports'.

In the modern world, however, blood sports are no longer respectable. The ancient connection between hunting and fishing and the provision of food has become incomprehensible to the inhabitants of the big cities where most people now live — eliminated by urbanisation itself, industrial farming, and the supermarket down at the mall. Bloodletting is shielded from the public gaze, and even in agricultural nations like Australia and New Zealand, whose economies are dependent on the annual slaughter of millions of animals, the idea of killing a deer or a duck is increasingly seen as barbaric.

Catching fish with a rod and line should, in theory, be no different. Blood is blood and dead is dead. But angling, unlike virtually every other form of hunting sport, delivers the victim to its captor alive. The choice is then up to the angler. He can put the fish back, absolving himself of the taint of blood, and evading the moral issue. Dead is not necessarily dead if the quarry is reprieved, and, coincidentally or not, the fashionable modern orthodoxy of catch-and-release has facilitated the notion that angling is essentially an innocent pursuit, a form of communion with nature. The modern angler is not a killer, or a crude harvester of protein. He is a sensitive fellow, light years removed from his gore-smitten, oafish ancestors, and the fish themselves — once routinely dispatched and eaten — have been refashioned as well. They are partners now with the anglers — playmates and collaborators in a rustic idyll of guilt-free recreation.

Angling, in other words, is a bona fide sport, like any other. Its participants engage in physical exercise and try to improve their performance. They are sportsmen, therefore, and sportswomen. They take part in competitions, just like rugby players or cricketers. There is even a world fly-fishing championship, sponsored by the airlines and rod manufacturers, and everyone else who thinks they might make a dollar.

This is not really surprising. The competitive instinct is never very far away. It seldom sleeps. There is hardly anything that people do that doesn't end up the subject of competition. We're brought up to think that competition is good: that it brings out the best in human beings and encourages them to excel. And maybe it does — or maybe we've let the notion get away on us to the point where it contaminates things that by nature should never be competitive.

The mere urge to compete, in any case, defines nothing. It is, in fact, compatible with outright lunacy. Consider ferret-legging, a rigorous 'sport' native to the North of England. There are no teams, just individual competitors. What happens is this. The blokes (they're all blokes, for reasons to become apparent) line up and tuck their trouser cuffs tightly into their socks. The trousers are equipped with stout belts, and when the whistle blows a set number of ferrets are dropped into each competitor's trousers, and the belts are tightened up. The winner, of course, is the bloke with the mad stoicism to put up with the punishment longest.

And while this is going on, believe it or not, down in the big tent at the other end of the village green the leggers' wives are submitting scones and jars of rhubarb chutney to a panel of judges who will sample them and eventually declare the winners. So you would have to say that the mere existence of competition is of little help in trying to define a 'sport'.

This train of thought was prompted by my rereading of a lovely old book on fishing — *Steelhead Paradise*, by an American, John F. Fennelly, published in Vancouver in 1963, and, as far as I know, only once reprinted. My own well-travelled copy — found in the general store in Kitimat, British Columbia, in 1969 — remains the only one I have ever seen, so it can hardly have been issued in big numbers. But it's a classic, nevertheless, evoking a time and a place and a moment in North American angling history just as it was passing forever.

Fennelly was a golf-playing investment banker who took up fly-fishing late in life. He describes the transition thus:

Golf had been my chief outdoor hobby
during all of my adult years, and at one
time I played with a very low handicap.
Unfortunately, I could see no satisfactory
future for my golf game. I realised that,
with each passing year, my long shots would
become shorter, and my handicap would
rise progressively with my age.

What fun it would be to find a new
hobby at which I could see improvement
rather than deterioration as the years
passed, and which I could enjoy virtually
as long as I could stand on two feet!

After considering several other
possibilities I finally concluded that fly-
fishing might be the answer to my prayer.
First, it would give me an outdoor life,
which I loved in almost any form. Second,
it would furnish as much physical exercise
as might be suitable for any particular
stage of life. And finally I realised that
it was an art that required delicacy of
skill rather than brute strength, and the
possibilities of which could never be
exhausted no matter how proficient one
might become.

Fennelly's analysis would be hard to beat. He starts from the fact of
physical decay and, conceding there is nothing to be done about
this, he moves ineluctably to angling — the one so-called sport
where youth, vigour and unbounded enthusiasm are no match
for old age, skill and cunning. And it is interesting to note that
Fennelly himself, throughout his book, seldom refers to fishing as
a sport, although as a successful banker and low-handicap golfer
he can hardly have been indifferent to the rewards of competition.

He may have been simply careless in this, for the terms he does use, such as 'hobby' or 'art', seem even less appropriate. But there is no doubt about what fishing meant to Fennelly. It became his life, and his years in British Columbia, when the wonderful rivers were hardly known, far eclipsed the sum of his younger years and yielded a matchless record of that fleeting time.

The pleasures of angling have been lauded often enough, but there are hazards too — especially in fly-fishing for trout. I remember an unfortunate I met years ago in a hut on the Worsley River, on the western shore of Lake Te Anau. He was an American — an East Coaster like Fennelly — and he had a passion to join some New York club whose entry condition was the landing of a ten-pound trout on a leader with a one-pound tippet.

I explained to him that this couldn't be done in a Fiordland river, and that his only chance was to hook his fish from a boat, well out in the lake, and then follow it around for a couple of days until it went to sleep, or died of boredom. But his life was solely fixated on the fulfilment of his crazed ambition. Every morning, no matter the weather, he disappeared upstream, climbing the cliffs and peering into the pools in search of the essential leviathan. He barely noticed the incomparable mountains, the siren beauty of the river, the wild, primaeval forest. All he cared about was his ten-pound trout. He is probably still down there somewhere, the ultimate martyr to the allure of angling.

This character, I'll admit, was an extreme case — but many trout fishermen have leanings in the same direction: they accumulate equipment, and books, and they neglect their jobs, and spend more and more time with confederates and accomplices, forsaking their wives and families.

Fishing is a curious business. It may begin as a hobby, or a recreation, or whatever you want to call it. But these are just words for our own bemusement, symbols elected to belie the chance that the game may change without warning, that the hobby may no longer be a hobby, if it ever was, and that days in the hills

Guilt-free recreation?

and the distant valleys in the domain of rivers in the thrall of trout may subvert all definitions. That definitions are immaterial, that they don't apply, and that without your noticing what was happening you are lost beyond recall.

THIRTEEN

Cookery

It was two o'clock and we were supposed to be going fishing, but Elmo was sitting on the porch with a book, and now he had opened a can of beer.

That Captain Cook has a lot to answer for, he said.

Eh?

Cook — the Captain — he was one devious bastard.

I knew what was coming, so I didn't respond. It has been like this ever since the Colonel took up with a bloke called Oodles, from the Anthropology Department. Oodles runs a course called 'The Essence of Indigeneity', and Elmo thinks he's a Maori now, on account of some recovered memory of jiggery-pokery between a dusky maiden and a sealer about two hundred years ago. It's all bollocks, of course, but once Oodles found out about the fictitious Maori princess Elmo was dog tucker. Elmo's whole world view has altered.

Yes, he continued. That Cook knew what he was doing. It was him that started the rot alright. He brought in trout, you know. He sailed up and down and released them all over the place and totally wiped out the native fish. Wiped out the mayfly as well, of course. Which the Maori — we Maori, I mean — traditionally used to eat.

Maori eating mayflies? I've never heard anything about that one.

They must have done. The old Maori were very ingenious, very resourceful people. If there were lots of mayflies they would have eaten them. But they can't now, of course, because the trout have cleaned them out.

It was pigs that Cook brought with him, Elmo, not trout. Trout were later, so you can't blame Cook on that one. And if you and your pals want to eat mayflies, go ahead. There's tons of them. You're a dry-fly man — what do you think you fish with?

That's irrelevant, said Elmo. You're prevaricating, as usual. Those trout bumped off all the native fish — the graylings and inangas and that sort of thing — which were treasures to us Maori. Trout are not treasures — they're invaders, they're colonisers. It was all part of the original plot.

By Captain Cook, I take it. Well, alright — but what about ducks, then? What about the mallard?

I don't quite follow . . .

Did Cook bring in the mallards as well?

Probably. I wouldn't put it past the bugger — mallards aren't native, are they?

No. But they've interbred with the grey ducks, and the grey ducks are natives, and therefore presumably treasures, and now the mallards and the greys are all mixed up. What do you think about that?

You're right. I'd completely forgotten about mallards. I'll have to talk to Oodles. Oodles will be very interested, and he'll know what to do alright. He'll probably want to wipe them out — just like the trout.

Wipe out the trout?

Yes. It would be very easy, apparently. Oodles has a scheme to put poison into the headwaters of every river in the country. Kill the lot. It would have to be a big operation, every river at the same time, so as to make sure of no survivors. Then the inanga would come back, and the lamprey, and the kumahora.

The kumawhata?

The kumahora. A beautiful, tragic fish. About ten pounds, average, Oodles says. They were blue on the top and green underneath, with red eyes and spikes on each side of the head. Rose to the fly and fought like marlin, and tasted a bit like pork. A real taonga, the old kumahora — and you've never even heard of it. Typical Pakeha ignorance.

Come on, Elmo, get a grip; you were a Pakeha yourself until six weeks ago. Forget about the bloody kumahora — Oodles is pulling your tit.

He wouldn't do that, would he?

Let's get back to the ducks. Your scheme won't work. How can you kill off the mallards when the grey ducks are all part-mallard? You'd have to kill them as well if you wanted to start over again — and if all the ducks were dead you'd have a bit of a problem.

Hmm, yes, that is a tricky one. That is definitely a curly one. See what I mean? Cook again. He set this up deliberately, and I bet he knew exactly what was going to happen. But don't worry, I'll talk to Oodles.

We started to throw our gear in the ute, but the Colonel was clearly troubled. He likes to have everything settled, no loose ends. He was a biologist before he became an economist, and he's a perfectionist in his own peculiar way, despite his lunatic tendencies. He went back to the house and came out with two cold beers.

We could breed back, he said, settling himself in the open door of the ute and pulling the tab from his beer.

Breed back?

Yes — like the aurochs. You remember the aurochs, don't you? It was a huge great ancestral cattle-beast that ran around wild in Europe until about 1672. Size of a truck, massive horns. Then they all died out.

And that was the end of that?

No, it wasn't. They bred them back. They bred up the most aurochs-looking cattle-beasts they could find, and bred again, and so on, and after a while the offspring started looking like aurochs. That's breeding back. I thought you'd have known about it.

I think I get it. You kill off all the ducks, except for a few that look a bit like grey ducks?

Exactly. That's breeding back. They've done it with all sorts of

146

Mayfly time: a four-pounder from Ardlussa.

animals, and we could do it with ducks. We could put pictures in the hunting licence: if it looks a bit grey, leave it alone, and if it looks too mallardy, blast it. You'd have grey ducks back in no time.

Has it occurred to you, Elmo, that there's been a bit of interbreeding on the human front as well?

Eh?

We're all interbred, all mixed up, everyone is. We're mongrels. You think I'm a European, but my genes are a kind of patchwork that started somewhere in Africa and ended up all over the world — and look at you. Two months ago you were a Pakeha, and now you think you're a Maori. If you were a duck you'd have to shoot yourself to tidy up the gene pool.

I think you're getting off the subject.

Well, it was you who brought it up. Breeding back, remember. That aurochs story was interesting, and I just wondered if you and Oodles had been considering any further initiatives in that line.

Elmo glared at me. You're a smart bastard, he said, but you're not going to wind me up. He heaved himself from the door of the ute and stretched his arms full width and shook his shoulders like a spaniel. He looked up in the air and then down at the ground. He raised his right boot and smashed his empty beer can into a perfect pancake. It's nearly three, he said. We're missing the best of the hatch.

We were, too — but not all of it. We drove down below the Ardlussa Bridge and across the paddocks to a big flat pool where a cloud of terns was swooping and diving, making a hell of a racket. It was hard to tell how many trout there were, with the rings of their rises overlaid by a scattershot of ternshit. But there were plenty. Elmo pulled up on a clay bank, close to the water.

There were drifts of mayflies coming down. They were all duns, the usual middle-sized, dark grey ones, rising in little clouds in the middle of the river.

Look, Elmo, I whispered. There's still a few left. You could get a feed if you wanted — you could take some back for Oodles.

But Elmo was no longer listening. He caught four trout, and I got five, all beauties — and all on mayflies.

FOURTEEN

Grub Time

Like many of the low-country Southland streams, the Mataura, for much of its course below the Nokomai Gorge, flows through a country of broad meadows and pastoral farmland. It meanders within wide-spaced flood banks, with shingle beaches on the insides of bends and, very often, a wall of willows opposite.

The trees stand shoulder to shoulder in places, their grey trunks tight-packed and immovable. They anchor the river banks and defy flood after flood, and in drought-time they provide shade and cover within the aqueous labyrinth of their roots. They are integral to the fishing of the Mataura.

Most years, when the snowmelt has gone and the river settled in its summer bed, the trout become more elusive. There are fewer rises to be seen along the flats, and the ripples are often deserted. Heat suffuses the shallows, and the mayfly nymphs retreat beneath their stones, and, day after day, the hot sun bakes the shingle. The Mataura is beautiful in these dog-days, sea-green and gently gliding beneath the plumage of the willows. And though the fishing is far from easy, the fish are still there, under those same sheltering willows. Down there in a cool, noonday twilight the trout lie idling, well fed from the bounty of springtime, and safe — safe until the madness of the willow-grubs.

It is a phenomenon of nature, this emergence: an eruption of life as prolific as the swarming of locusts or the schooling of salmon, or the mad migration of lemmings. But it is witnessed only by anglers and trout, for a willow-grub is a tiny thing — no bigger than a grain of rice.

The grubs leave their cocoons when the weather warms up, emerging from their tumour-like homes in the innumerable leaves of the willows, and, tumbling from their perches, they fall into the river. On windless days, with the sun high, a drizzle of fat grubs sifts constantly down through the foliage, and the trout, stationed beneath, feed methodically, hour upon hour. This is a fine torment to the angler: fish rising close to hand, confidently sipping, tantalisingly audible, and yet, beneath the impenetrable tangle of willow branches, utterly unreachable.

When a warm wind blows, however — as it often does — the possibilities are excitingly different. The willow-grubs no longer fall straight down through the trees, but sail out on lateral trajectories determined by the strength and direction of the wind. Many of them are blown completely clear of the willows, and the fish then venture from their cover and forage out into open water, very visible and wonderfully exposed. On the best days, with the wind just right, whole squadrons of grubs are flung across the stream, gust after gust, and the trout in their greed forget their instinctive caution. Magnificent trout, seldom seen by daylight, dart boldly around, chasing each other, chasing grubs, oblivious to danger.

This is a rare kind of fishing. It seems, at first sight, to be a promise of dry-fly heaven. How can one go wrong? Just look at those trout! Four of them, lined up right there — no — five. And there's another one! There, goddammit! See — it rose again, right there. Christ, what a monster. That one's mine, Alvin. No, it's mine, I tell you. Out of the way, Alvin — that's my fish!

Tourist anglers, especially, often become delirious on first encountering the willow-grub. Here, at last, is the great day they have been waiting for since first they took up a fly-rod. Dreams are about to be realised. Those fish are dead. They're on the bank, or as good as. Those fish won't spook. They can't be put down. That one swam straight towards you and sucked down a willow-grub so close you could count the ribs of his gills. Oh, boy, this is it. Get the camera ready, Alvin. Stay calm. Stay calm! Count to fifty — slowly. Breathe easy. OK. Now, what's the proper fly?

The proper fly. Ah, yes — the proper fly.

The willow-grub is simplicity itself. It is a quarter-inch corrugated cylinder of yellow-green grease with a tiny, spherical, dark-brown head. It is a far less complex organism than, say, a mayfly imago, and it is ridiculously easy to copy — just a few turns of floss on a size-sixteen hook is near-perfect. Attach one of these to your leader and, in theory, you are in business.

The first time I tried this — on the Mataura — was classic. There were the trout, all in a line and rising like they were tied together. I waded in behind the last one and made a perfect delivery of my newfangled floss-bodied grub. The trout took it without hesitation — and so did the next one, and the next one. It was simplicity itself. The trout were as lambs to the slaughter, and I hauled each one downstream the moment it was hooked, away from the others, and caught the whole row, like clockwork. It was a ridiculous rout, and, like many another happy ignoramus, I thought I had solved the problem of the willow-grub.

The following weekend, fully confident, I waded in behind a line of trout and made a nice cast to the tail-ender. It kept on feeding, rising every twenty seconds or so, but totally ignoring my grub. I decided maybe it had been hooked before, and moved up to the next one. But the result was exactly the same, and after an hour they were all still feeding and I hadn't had a touch. And the same thing happened for the rest of the day. There were trout behind every willow tree, but I was completely skunked.

I was puzzled, but I wasn't dismayed. I was sure I was nearly

A willow-grubber.

there, and I set about changing the pattern, a little at a time, convinced that a subtle alteration in shade, or a whisker of hackle, or a different-shaped hook, would give me the answer — the ultimate, foolproof grub. And I thought I had cracked it once or twice, knocking out whole rows of fish just like I had the first time.

Seasons passed, of varying fortune. Sometimes the trout were easy, rekindling foolish delusions, but finally I came to understand that there is no answer to the problem of the willow-grub. Every 'answer' is temporary, and what works like magic today will be sure to fail tomorrow.

It was a white-hot noonday in February, with the wind from the west, and Dougal and I had been fishing for an hour or more to a pod of impervious three-pounders. Grubs sailed by in flotillas, and the trout rose with seeming abandon. We cast up to them, down to them, and directly across to their rhythmically emerging snouts, but we never had a take — not even to our latest 'answer'.

I remember reading somewhere, said Dougal, that in situations like this you need to think like a trout.

He reeled in, removed his futile willow-grub, and tied on a large contraption made of camel-hair, tinsel and cellophane. It was about the size of a lemon, with the bronzed glitter of a mutant cicada. He got this apparatus airborne and shot it out across the glassy, pale-green water.

It landed with a notable splash, nicely positioned, I thought, to scare the whole line of feeding fish. The first one turned tail and disappeared, but the next — of course — came up and seized the lemon. It jumped once, then tried to get under the willows, but Dougal gave it no slack and soon it was flapping on the shore.

When all else fails, in willow-grub time, try thinking like a trout.

FIFTEEN

Fly-fish

Once, slogging through an endless swamp in the Grebe River valley, tormented by flies and weighed down by a leaden pack, I watched a helicopter fly low overhead. It was an old Bell machine, similar to those used by the Americans in the Korean War, and familiar to later generations from the TV programme *M*A*S*H*.

The two occupants were clearly visible as it passed, and the pilot waved briefly before banking sharply for a line of tall trees and vanishing round a bend in the river. And then silence again, the valley as undisturbed as if the chopper had never existed.

There is a certain masochistic pleasure in living for a week on what you can carry on your back. The Iron Men of the past all seemed to thrive on it, lugging great swags of ammunition, oatmeal, hard tack and rice into the remotest wilderness, and returning, invariably, with a huge rack of antlers strapped atop a ton of venison.

But it's a pleasure that eventually palls. Once the essentials have been crammed into the pack — minimal and almost inedible food, spare clothes, cooking gear, sleeping bag, tent, and equipment for whatever you are intending to do — there isn't much room for anything else, even if you can bear the load. And the further you go the harder it gets. A helicopter is the ultimate answer, but helicopters are reserved for the rich.

Years ago, when Fiordland was our happy hunting ground, Turner and I bought an aluminium boat and a forty-horsepower Johnson. Immediately our prospects expanded as vast swathes of country, hitherto beyond reach, suddenly became accessible. The great southern lakes — Hauroko, Monowai, Manapouri and Te Anau — were transformed from barriers to highways. And no longer were we limited to the meagre contents of a pack: the boat could carry anything that two or even three people might possibly want, skimming past forests and cliffs to distant shores and Forestry huts, provisioned for weeks — and not just with the bare essentials.

North of Fiordland, however, where the big lakes are ringed by roads, there was no advantage in using the boat. Many of the tributary valleys had four-wheel-drive tracks, but to reach the prime territory where these tracks ran out it was still essential to get out and slog on foot for two or three hours at least. Once again, to find new country, we were restricted to the contents of a pack. Turner was philosophic: there's no way round it, he said. We either do it, or stay at home.

We did it, reluctantly, for years. We left town after work on Fridays and drove far into the mountains, camping by moonlight at the ends of dirt roads, and labouring on, bleary, in the morning. It kept us fit, but it was punishing work, and I still hankered for a way to reach the places that we could never get to on foot — the ultimate, faraway folds of the Alps, and the jungles that lay beyond the snowfields. There were easier ways, I was sure of it.

All over the South Island high country, in almost every valley inhabited by deer, are the traces of disused airstrips. They are nearly invisible, except from the air — faint parallel lines etched on the spines of tussock ridges, on river terraces and grassy flats, in clearings among scrub and beech trees. They are relics of a time now almost forgotten, when the most efficient way to lift venison from the bush was in the belly of a Piper Cub.

Cubs — and the Cessna 180s that followed them — were able to operate from the most primitive of airfields, and back in the 1960s they were perfect for the New Zealand backblocks. For ten years or more they revolutionised the venison business, retrieving the carcasses of innumerable deer, and adding a chapter of latter-day banditry to the saga of bush aviation. But when the first helicopters arrived, the planes were history. They were competing with machines that could land anywhere, that didn't need an airstrip at all.

Here, I figured, was the answer. Helicopters may have taken over the venison trade, but the old strips were still there, and many of them must still be usable. All I needed was a surplus Cub, at the right price, and I could get into some wonderful country. I could take a passenger and plenty of gear. Never again need I haul a pack.

But Cubs, I soon discovered, had become very far from cheap. They had gone from being obsolete to desirable, and a brisk trade had sprung up in rebuilding them for sale to rich collectors in America. Even the worst of non-flying wrecks, fabric rotten and engines long dead, were worth many times what they had cost when new. And there were other snags I hadn't considered: high maintenance costs, official bloody-mindedness, and the need for a pilot's licence. Cubs, I was eventually forced to conclude, were no longer a viable option, and I gave up dreaming about aeroplanes.

One day in the late 1990s, on some bouncy water near Cattle Flat, I met two Americans from Idaho. Their names were Geronimo and Redeye, and we stopped for a yarn and the usual lies about the fishing. The Yanks were good anglers and had caught a few — including a four-and-a-half-pounder, they said — much bigger than anything in the rivers back home. We compared flies and tactics and talked about things we had seen and done, and eventually the conversation came around to the perennial problem of escaping the mob and getting into the bush without paying to hire a JetRanger, or busting your back with a pack. It turned out that these Yanks (who were both about my age — the post-pack-bearing age) had considered the same situation and come to the same conclusion: what they needed was an aeroplane 'that could land on a dime', but which cost a lot less than a rebuilt Cub.

They had found one — but it wasn't a normal, factory-built plane. It was a new invention called a kit plane. 'Remember those little balsa-wood models you built when you were a kid?' said Geronimo. 'It's the same idea, only bigger. You get everything you need in the kit, for a fraction of the price of an ordinary plane — and there are hundreds of them to pick from.'

This story sounded too good to be true. But the Americans reckoned they'd been everywhere in this two-seat plane they put together in their garage. 'We flew up to British Columbia the fall before last,' said Redeye. 'Landed on gravel bars on the Skeena;

caught salmon, shot a bear. Cost us nothing but the tag for the bear and the price of gas and food.' They kept the plane in a home-built hangar on their local airfield, and their next big trip, they said, would be for steelhead in Alaska. 'I'll send you some literature soon as we get home,' promised Redeye. 'Without a kit plane, Dave, you ain't living.'

I phoned the local aero club as soon as I got back to town. Yes, they'd heard of kit planes alright — apparently there were lots of them over in America. And no, as far as they knew there were none in the Otago vicinity. But I could hire a Cessna, if I wanted, and they knew of a nice Cub in Queenstown — all it needed was a new engine and wings, and it was a bargain at $100,000. And then, a month or so later, a thick parcel arrived from Idaho.

Five Hundred and Thirty-seven Aircraft You Can Build, it said on the cover of a fat, glossy catalogue.

There were aircraft of every shape and form: helicopters, gyrocopters, monoplanes, biplanes, even full-scale replica Spitfires. I read the catalogue from cover to cover, incredulous that such a revolution in aviation had happened without my noticing. The choice of machines was bewildering, and in comparing the data on powerplants, take-off distances, and rates of climb, I quite forgot the original reason as to why I wanted an aeroplane. Flight itself — the intoxicating vision of getting into the air — had become the objective, rather than a means to an end, and nothing that flew, I eventually decided, could possibly come close to a beautiful little two-seat jet called the BD-10, 'buildable in the average home workshop'.

The BD-10 was a lulu. It used an army-surplus jet engine (readily available and very cheap, according to the kit manufacturer), and was described as having a 'military fighter performance', while remaining 'perfectly simple to fly'. The figures were astronomic, with the standard home-built BD-10 capable of 926 mph in level flight, and able to reach ten thousand feet 'within one minute of releasing the brakes'.

This, I thought, is the berries. Why fart around with obsolete Austers and broken-down Piper Cubs when I can have a brand-new supersonic jet? I'll dump the old MG and the motorbikes and clear a bit of space in the workshop. Once the kit arrives — say six weeks from now — I'll have it whacked together in no time at all. And then it's just a matter of getting checked out at the aero club and I'm in business. So I sent away twenty dollars for a 'full information package'.

This took some weeks to arrive. Meanwhile I organised the workspace and thought about the fun I was going to have when my BD-10 was up and operational. Calm summer mornings at the airfield. A fresh-brewed coffee and — just one blistering minute later — Mach 1.2 at ten thousand feet! Not bad, really, for a box of bits put together in the garage.

The possibilities were amazing. In a frisky mood I might skim up the Alps and across Cook Strait to Ohakea, give the Air Force boys a couple of sonic booms at rooftop height, and scoot home again before they managed to scramble some obsolete transport tub or Vietnam-era chopper. Nothing would be able to catch me — not even a reactivated Skyhawk. Oh yes, this was definitely going to beat commuting to the pub in the Ford Sierra.

But there were some rather obvious drawbacks, as the nicely illustrated information package was shortly to remind me. The BD-10, to begin with, drank kerosene at a furious rate, and the military-surplus jet engine needed a lot of expert maintenance, so it would be an expensive little brute to run. And then there was the back-country capability, which, with a landing-roll of about a mile, was strictly non-existent. I'd need a major airfield, not an acre of thistles in a creekbed. It was sadly plain that a baby jet, whatever its blood-curdling hoonish charms, was useless as a bush plane. I would have to reconsider.

There were numerous Cub-type planes in the catalogue, and since most of them had a similar performance, I settled in the end for the same two-seat microlight monoplane that Geronimo and Redeye had built, and had told me about originally. It was called an Avid Mark IV, and cruised at a leisurely seventy knots (no playing games with the Air Force). But it could climb at forty-five degrees and 'land on a dime'. It could take me where

I wanted to go. So I contacted the New Zealand agent and had a word with the man at the bank.

Building the thing was easy, if seriously time-consuming. All the bits, as promised, were in one big box, the two-cylinder engine included, and it went together very much like an oversized model. It had a steel-tube fuselage and wooden ribs with aluminium spars for the wings. The whole lot was covered with Ceconite — a new, heat-shrink fabric that eliminated all the wizardry required in the days of linen and cotton. Wrinkles and sags disappeared at a pass of the smoothing-iron, leaving a taut, immaculate surface. A few coats of dope — yes, the same stuff as used on the old balsa-wood jobs — and there was my gleaming new ersatz Cub: blue, green, silver, and lovely.

I sent some papers off to Wellington, explaining that I was ready to fly, and a bloke came down, looked at the plane, and told me to go ahead — the lack of obstruction or bureaucratic bungling being as pleasing as it was unexpected. So I hitched the Avid to the back of the ute, wings folded alongside the fuselage, and towed it over to the Taieri airfield.

An aeroplane, I soon found, is not like a car. Its responses, at the whim of the air, seem more animal than mechanical. One moment it is docile, behaving exactly as its pilot intends, and the next it has a mind of its own. Nor is it constrained by the infrastructure of roads and rules that make modern driving so maddening. It moves with the freedom of an aerial boat in a three-dimensional ocean. It reacts to the wind — speeding up, slowing down, moving in unexpected directions. This is the real joy of flying, never to repeat the same journey, to detour past cloud banks or mountain peaks, to see new country (or familiar country from a new perspective); to savour, skipping easily from valley to valley, a delicious release from that crawling domain of speed limits, breath tests and cops.

Many of my old friends were dubious about my new obsession. They were reluctant to believe that something I built in the garage could ever get off the ground, or be anything but lethal if it did. But what did they know? The plane did exactly what

An easier way to the backblocks.

Landing strip at Cotter's on the Dingle.

it was supposed to do: it took off and landed in the tiniest of paddocks and climbed like a little rocket. I spent most of my time at the aero club, picking the brains of the other pilots and flying whenever I could. And as the hours built up I gained confidence.

It is nine o'clock in the morning, at the height of the green-beetle season, and Turner and I are perched in the sky, heading north from Oturehua. The Manuherikia valley reels slowly behind as we climb towards the Omarama Saddle. Far away to the north is the silver disc of Lake Ohau, and immediately ahead the blue vein of the Ahuriri. The air is smooth and the wings steady, and we are moving, according to the airspeed indicator, at eighty-five miles an hour. It doesn't feel like that. It feels, in the confines of our little cabin, that we are sitting still, and only the tiny plume of dust from a car, half a mile below on the gravel road, dropping behind, confirms our motion.

Turner is not entirely at ease. He examines the instruments and looks nervously at the wings and struts. The windscreen is vibrating, he says. Quite normal, I assure him. The doors are vibrating too, he says, and there's a funny noise coming from the engine.

It's Turner's first flight in the Avid, and he's been listening to the doomsters. And it's true that the engine sounds funny — it's a two-stroke, like a lawnmower engine. It emits a high-pitched whine, not a reassuring rumble like the standard aero engines. And of course he knows that the whole machine came out of a box of bits.

The Ahuriri glitters in the morning light, and the high mountains draw gradually closer. We need a bit more height so I open the throttle and the motor yowls at full blat till we level off again, but Turner makes no further comment or complaint, and in a few minutes the Birchwood Lagoons are under our wings, close to the hills on the west. There are two cars by the road and anglers beside them, looking up.

The Ahuriri is a famous trout stream, and Turner and I have fished here often over the years, sleeping out in the tussock or camping in the hut at the forest's edge near the confluence with Canyon Creek. We are approaching it now, banking over a big, oval pool where the two streams meet. It's tempting: we could spiral down and land on a beach, and maybe catch a ten-pounder. But there's a road right up the valley, and every year there are more and more anglers.

To the west, in a steep, bush-filled gully, is an old stock-track that leads to a low pass in the crest of the range. We've been here as well, on foot, lugging our packs over this same pass and down to the next river — the Dingleburn. How easy it seems, from above, and I tip the aeroplane on its side, and spin around to look back down the gully and into the forest. The track is hidden beneath the canopy of the trees, but clearly visible where it climbs through the tussock and across the bare flanks of scree, the zigzagged legacy of decades of sweat — Turner's and mine included.

There's no sweating this time. The ground drops away as we skim over the pass and into the head of the Dingle. High mountains fill the sky ahead and above, black Alps and ice, and four thousand feet beneath our wheels is a tiny triangular arena of tussock, gold in the sun, surrounded by the dark drapery of the bush. There was an airstrip there in the old deerhunting days, but it was wiped out by floods, and the next one, about six miles away, is hidden round a bend in the river. From this height we can glide the whole way.

It is very quiet without the motor. The propeller windmills and stops. There is no vibration and almost no sound — only the hiss of the wind. The mountains loom close beneath the blue arch of the sky, and the skin of the plane, tough as leather but paper-thin, flexes with every movement of the controls. Gravity changes from moment to moment, pressing hard, easing off, sometimes reversing. We are riding the air like a hawk, riding it down, and there is a sense of being almost part of the machine, feeling each tremor of the airframe, inhabiting it like a bird its feathers. We sail close to the mountainside and then away, over the river, over the bush, and then back again, silent, watching our shadow on the floor of the valley, watching the altimeter unwind. Every detail of the river is clear, and there's just enough wind near the ground to move the grass on the flats. It's blowing upstream: we can glide straight in.

The airstrip is seldom used now, although it is not a bad strip. It lies next to the river, on the right bank where a small tributary comes in — a piece of flat ground with the wheel-ruts of long-gone Piper Cubs fading into the tussock. There's a single beech tree at the upper end — a handy marker, and we are just over it, slowing and flaring, about to touch down, when Turner spots a posse of anglers. Three of them, he says. No, four.

There's no point in landing. Power on again and we rocket straight ahead, over the ridge at the end of the strip and then pull round, the aircraft skidding, wings vertical, hard round and across the little bunch of fishermen on the river bank. Turner waves and they wave back.

We could go on down to Cotter's Creek, a few minutes away, and land on a terrace at the head of the gorge, and fish back up through a stony flat that used to hold lots of trout. But it was ripped apart three years ago, in a monster flood, and it's hardly likely to have recovered so soon. The Dingle is no-go, for today at least. But it's still early in the morning, and we have plenty of gas.

The next valley over is the Hunter. The mountains in between seem pretty high, and there are no obvious passes in the skyline. Turner finds the map, and we keep on climbing, levelling out every now and again to let the engine cool off, and get to six thousand feet in just over six minutes. The perspective is different now, but not a lot better — still an impassable, jagged barrier. We can keep going up, but according to Turner we're high enough. He squints at the map and points to a side-creek, and, sure enough, when we fly up it there's a gap at the top, with steep bluffs on either side. Another five hundred feet and we're above them, with clear sky in front and the Hunter valley below, and Lake Hawea a silver mirror in the sun.

The Hunter is big — many times bigger than the Dingle. It runs straight from the Alps in a great, open valley, and in summertime, when the water is low, it meanders in ripples and shallow pools through a braided bed of grey sand and pebbles. There are trout far into the headwaters, and when the mayflies are scarce in the long, warm days they forage and grow fat on a rich drift of beetles and hoppers and cicadas.

But nothing is permanent in the Hunter. It floods every spring — huge floods that tear the bed apart and push a plume of silt and soil and uprooted trees far out into the lake. Everything changes. New pools are formed, new ripples and braids and backwaters. Yet the trout have somehow adapted to this seasonal destruction of their habitat, and even the mayflies hang on, burrowing deep beneath the migrating stones, ineradicable.

We are orbiting in motionless air, a mile above the river. Small, wispy clouds are floating in the sky not far below, and as we bank to the north, away from the lake, the whole valley has an appearance of completeness in itself, like a painting. The world beyond is invisible, and the river flats and dark-green forested slopes are bathed in a dazzling, undifferentiated light, enclosed in a rim of mountains, bounded by the dome of the sky.

There are several good airstrips in the valley, and a few dicey ones, and the shingle beaches can often be used as well. At long intervals there are huts — old Forest Service relics of a time when the valley was full of deer, but there is no wisp of woodsmoke from any of them. The air is so still that the plane flies by itself for ten minutes or more, gliding evenly with the motor shut off, and on either side the forests sweep up in a perfect vee to the snowline. The ground slips past, coming closer, and the river swirls in a single course through small clearings among fingers of the bush. We are tree-height from the ground, the motor running again, and the last place we can get down in one piece is on Forbes Flat, just minutes ahead.

The forest ends in the Alps. Icefalls. Snowfields. Glaciers. A narrow gorge yawns directly below, and the bush is a blur, not far from our wingtips. Thermal air is rising from the sun-warmed rocks, lifting in bubbles and bouncing us over the stunted scrub along the rim of the gorge. A last barrier of trees, and then, beyond a wide, rough gully, the vague threshold of the strip. We are over the trees, dropping past them, nose-high, slipping and sinking towards the boulder bed of the gully. Throttle closed: we are high enough. The wheels hit, and bounce, and hit again, a short bumpy ride. The propeller kicks and stops, and Turner climbs out and waters the tussock, and is relieved in more ways than one.

There are two trout feeding in the only pool on the flat. They're not big, but they're very busy, and we watch them for a while, standing on the bank in the sweet, stubby grass, pleased with the warmth of the summer air and the darting fish and the enveloping silence of the valley. We are miles and miles from anywhere, from any road, or house, or human. Neither of us is carrying a pack.

SIXTEEN

Angus

New Zealand, paradoxically, is not at all an easy place to learn the art of freshwater fishing. We have rivers and lakes in abundance, and trout still living in most of them, yet, when it comes to learning the basic skills and hooking that vital first fish, New Zealand can be very tough.

The main reason for this is obvious. Apart from trout, and in some places salmon, we have hardly anything else that grows big enough to be worth catching on rod and line. Unlike Europe or North America, a beginner can't practise on easy stuff (so-called coarse fish), and move gradually up to salmonids.

I was reminded of this problem last February, when my nephew, Angus, came over from England. Angus is seven, and was armed with a new rod and reel and an unshakeable belief that New Zealand's rivers were rife with ravenous trout just waiting to tangle with Angus. I could hardly disillusion him with the sober truth, so I said OK, we'll go and have a look at the Mataura.

It is many years since I tried to teach anyone fishing, and I don't recall, even then (when the fish were more plentiful and far easier to catch), that my efforts were very successful. And I hadn't used a spinning rod either, for decades, but I supposed that, like riding a bicycle, it was something you don't forget.

We took off on a calm, sunny morning, and flew south and west, over the wide blue Clutha and the rolling green hills and the Pomahaka's brown, rocky bed. (This was a cunning plan on my part, since, I reasoned, even if we caught nothing, Angus would enjoy the flying.)

He did. Perched on three fat cushions he examined the rivers intently, informing me each time he thought he had spotted a fish. There were plenty of them, he said — so many big trout, in fact, that a couple of dozen of them were as good as dead already.

Well, you can guess more or less what happened. For the first hour or two we were fully engaged in improving Angus's casting. He fired out lures at random, occasionally hitting the Mataura. He got the hang of it, though, and soon he was making long shots to the far bank and mostly avoiding the snags. But there were no trout, of course, with the heat of the day and the river so low, and all I could do was keep up the fiction that success was just round the corner. Good, Angus, I said. Very good cast. Just put another one right in there; there must be a trout in there — in fact I know there's a trout in there. I saw it last week. It's a big one.

The trout remained unresponsive, and dinner that evening was sausages and bacon with Wattie's baked beans, which, Angus declared, were every bit as good as the famous baked beans that he ate all the time in England. They'd be awesome with trout, he said, innocently, leaving me no room for manoeuvre. Alright, I said. All-bloody-right, Angus. You can find out for yourself tomorrow night. Trout and beans tomorrow, or bust.

Angus.

The next day was a golden day, heat shimmering from the bleached schist-stones and mallard hiding in the willows. It was a day for lying under a tree with a book, sipping a nice cold beer. There were no flies on the water, and no fish, no sign of life, not even a circling harrier-hawk in the thermals over the barley. It was hopeless, but I couldn't say so.

Mid-afternoon, and still hot. We kept going upstream, Angus still doggedly casting. That's good, I said from time to time. Any minute now. Just drop another one beside that big rock. Reel just a little bit slower.

Angus cast again. The lure sailed out in a perfect parabola, and fell close to a high clay bank, and sank into the pale-green water. Angus retrieved unhurriedly, watching for the glint of the spinner. And there it was — and there, miraculously, behind it, swam a big, live, beautiful trout.

Look at that, Angus, I whispered. Look, look there, it's a trout. But Angus had seen it already. He was standing very still, transfixed, watching the fish. Everything had stopped: Angus, the trout, the day. The reel had stopped, too, and the spinner lay inert on the bottom.

But the day was suddenly different. Trout were no longer make-believe things. They were under the banks, and hidden behind rocks — they were everywhere. They were clever, too, but one of them, at least, had nearly been caught. Tremendous possibilities abounded, and now every cast was a hopeful one. Pool after pool, hundreds of casts through the long afternoon, and then, at last, two trout darting from the shadows.

They were both the same size: big enough. They slowed, almost nudging the lure. They slid across the river, side by side, into the shallows, bellies on the sand. Then, simultaneously, they whirled and fled in twin eruptions of silt. They were almost at Angus's feet.

We walked back downstream, crossing and recrossing at the tail of each pool. There were small clouds of midges in the breathless air, and a few stray duns were emerging. We would have to come back, said Angus — back to those same places where those same trout would still surely be, and this time he would catch them. They had been so close, just another few feet, and . . .

A trout rose, close to the bank, in water no more than shin-deep. Its dorsal fin was just visible, and then the whole dark line of its back as it took something unseen from the surface. There was no wind, no drag: it was an easy place. One cast with a dun was all it would take, but a spinning-lure would be useless. Do you see him, Angus?

Yes.

That's dinner, I said.

And later, with beans, it was.

SEVENTEEN

Mayflies

When fly-fishing first became fashionable, in the days of Queen Victoria, it was the fly that was the focal point, rather than the method of delivery. And the fly in question was not just any old fly (or gnat, or hopper, or bumblebee) that a trout might care to eat. Perish the thought. The fly in question was the mayfly, which, the purists held, should be fished only in its aerial form, and never underwater.

But who remembers this nowadays? In the course of a century our perceptions have changed, and the mad controversies of Victorian times — when dry-fly men spurned all association with their renegade colleagues who fished the nymph — seem to us inexplicable.

We have come a long way from that tweed-clad, uptight era. We are more indulgent now, more tolerant. We no longer insist, or care, what kind of missile our fellow anglers attach to their leaders. Anything goes — as long as it works. New 'flies' appear every season, resembling no insect that ever existed. New nymphs are minted, each smaller and denser than the last. Size fourteen — the old mayfly standard — is a big fly these days, almost obsolete, and the experts are down to hook number twenty-eight — the size of a streptococcus, wrapped in depleted uranium.

Trout will eat almost anything — smaller trout if they can catch them. They are opportunists, perennially hungry, and worms, mice, cicadas, beetles and wasps are just as acceptable as the classic aquatic insects. Examine the gut of your average trout and what do you find among the assorted invertebrates? Feathers and stones, sticks and leaves — whatever came down in the current. Trout are not very particular. They will take a lead ball, painted bright green and containing a hook. They are easily fooled by the beadheaded bombs that have now become standard equipment, and the exact imitation of stream-born insects — the trout's most common natural food — is no longer considered essential. There is no need, in fact, to be constrained by nature at all. Novelty rules, and, for many anglers, the old connection between trout and mayflies has been largely forgotten. Purists are a dying race.

I was thinking about this the other week while fishing the Waikaia with my old mates Two-Pies and Dougal. It was a drizzly day and the fishing was slow, so we split up to cover the water more effectively. Two-Pies went upstream and Dougal went down, while I worked my way through a nice long stretch of fast water. I hooked one fish briefly, and then another, which I landed. The rain got heavier, and I was near the top of the reach when I saw a mayfly popping out of the river in front of me. It stood out clearly in the pattering rain, a big black dun with glossy wings. It sat up and wobbled a little, and jumped around, and then all of a sudden there were dozens of them. I looked at my watch. It was one thirty-four.

I put on a Cul de Canard — a four-feather version that floated high and looked a dead ringer for the naturals. The duns were now thick on the water, sailing along and flexing their wings. It

Prime water on the Waikaia.

was an explosion of life, a feast of flies, and I watched and waited, but no fish rose.

I went up past the ripple to the flat above. It was deep and slow-flowing with head-high clay banks and a big backwater behind a gravel shoal — part of an old river channel, with solid willows along one bank. The backwater was stippled with mayflies, and a great trout was cruising confidently around, sampling them at leisure.

Ambushing the fish was easy. The willows provided a perfect screen, and all I had to do was drop the Cul de Canard directly on to the water. The trout was down deep, near the bottom. It moved along slowly towards me. Then it paused and pivoted in a little disturbance of silt and swam straight up to take a high-floating dun, right beside my imitation. It was a very odd rise — the fish standing on its tail with its whole head and shoulders pushed out of the water. Then it sank back and rolled over and went down again to repeat the performance. This time it was my turn, and I was looking right down the trout's gullet when it took my fly, and I could count the gill-rakers on each side of its throat as I waited for it to close its mouth and roll over.

It was brilliant. It was like fishing in slow motion. The trout was halfway to the bottom when I set the hook, and after that it was mayhem. But I had a heavy tippet and I held on tight, and for all the trout's efforts it never managed to get me under a snag. It was a five-pound female, very beautiful but too big to keep.

Things were a bit post-coital after all that excitement. There were a few small fish out in the mainstream, and a bigger one in ankle-deep water that I nearly stepped on. Then the hatch died out and Two-Pies appeared, grinning in the rain, and we ambled off downstream in search of Dougal.

There is a mystery in the hatching of mayflies. Some signal occurs that we can't detect, and the ripe nymphs swim away from the riverbed. They punch through the surface and struggle out of their nymphal jackets. They usually do this at the same time, up and down the river, and I've heard it said you can set your watch by the famous hatches on the English chalk streams.

And so it was in this case. The flies had appeared at one-thirty, give or take a few minutes, and during the next half-hour we caught just one fish each. But the weird thing was that the flies were of different species. The duns that Dougal and Two-Pies had seen were tiny, pale-grey things, while mine were twice as big, and black as charcoal.

There is no end to mayfly mysteries. Two-Pies thinks that they are very highly evolved, with phenomenal cerebral capacities. They may be tiny but according to Two-Pies their social structures are as complex as anything developed by humans. They have different tribes and races and subcultures and live in separate ghettos, and communicate, he thinks, by a form of telepathy — which is how the hatches are synchronised. The big black tribe must have intercepted the signals of the little grey buggers and decided to join the hatch for the hell of it.

As a theory this is hard to beat. It explains all the data and leaves no loose ends, and the fact that it is almost certainly crap is neither here nor there until somebody comes up with a better one. Not that I give a monkey's.

The rivers we have left are beautiful, but many of the people along their banks have ceased to play any useful part in their ecology. Flotsam of a burdened planet, they are walking inventories of the same technological arrogance that has stuffed up most of the fishing. Trout-bums in Gore-Tex from the four corners of the Earth, laden with exotic hardware. Why not fish with grenades?

The old blokes in the tweed jackets were right all along. They were anglers, not touring technologists. They recognised the essential and organic link in the strange business that is fly-fishing. They knew that without the mayfly there is no magic in our haunting of rivers — that these tiny spinners and duns, above all God's creatures, unite us with our prey. Spawn of air as well as water, they connect, in their changeling perfection, the isolate domains of the angler and the trout, the lives of the hunters and the hunted. Nothing else comes close, and nothing ever will, as long as fresh water flows.

EIGHTEEN

Carol

The original plan, when I built the aeroplane, was that Carol would come flying with me. It would be family transport, not just an accessory to fishing and hunting — and so it was, for a while.

T hen, coming back from a weekend at Big Bay, we hit some turbulence near the head of the Red Pyke valley. There was no indication it was going to be rough. The wind had been a light sea breeze when we took off from the beach, and rather than go down the Pyke to the Hollyford — my usual route — I decided to do a scenic tour through the Simonin Pass into the Cascade, and round the west face of Mount Aspiring.

Turbulence is no fun in any aeroplane, even a passenger jet. But the smaller and lighter the machine the worse it is, and planes don't come much smaller and lighter than the Avid.

We were approaching the pass, flying over the barren moonscape of the Red Hills, when suddenly the nose went down, and without any warning we were heading for the ground in a vertical dive and going very fast. I pulled back on the stick, which didn't produce any noticeable effect. The crest of the pass was coming up, and then we seemed to hit a brick wall, still a hundred feet clear of the rocks. We shot forward in the straps and then there was a powerful punch from below and we were soaring back up into empty air.

Nothing in my training had prepared me for this. The plane yawed and bucked and rolled on its back, tossed in tempests of wind that shook the airframe and warped the wings, and would, any second I thought, rip the machine apart. There was no fixed relation to the earth or sky. One moment we were flying on an even keel and the next we were upside down, tossed like a cork in a fountain. Mountainsides came close, and then disappeared, and there was nothing I could do but play with controls that seemed to have been disconnected.

Four minutes later we came out of it — the longest four minutes of my life. The battering ceased as suddenly as it had started, and the snowfields and valleys and peaks reassumed their normal relation to the sky. But the damage had been done. If we get out of this, Carol said. If we get home alive, I'll never go flying again.

I flew the Avid for ten years after that, and although there were times when I wished I was back on the ground, they were nothing compared with that four minutes in the Simonin Pass.

Then I built another aeroplane: a RANS S7, a modern version of the Piper Cub. It was more powerful than the Avid, and could carry more gear and fly a bit faster and still land on short, rough strips. And when I fitted a special undercarriage and big, soft tyres it was the ultimate back-country bus.

Carol was still terrified of flying. I explained to her that the RANS was a different machine, and she ought to give it a try. It was stronger and much more stable, I said. Turbulence was nothing to this aeroplane — and anyway I was more on the ball these days, and I could spot turbulence miles away. But Carol was having none of that.

The RANS was everything I had always wanted, and I flew more often than ever. I hardly used the car, except to go into town, or drive over to the airfield. I found new places to fish and hunt — up in the mountains and over on the Coast, and we had an endless supply of venison and trout, and occasionally blue cod and crayfish. I took Two-Pies and Turner and the rest of the boys, but Carol stayed resolutely at home.

Then one morning she came out to the airfield. I was going to the Dingleburn for an overnighter and was checking the oil and the tyre pressures, and topping up the tanks, and when I was finished I made some coffee and we sat in the sun watching the club planes take off and land. It was a beautiful, late-summer morning, and the little planes buzzed round the circuit, whistling low past the hangar and over the fence and touching down on the grass. But it was time to go, if I wanted to do any fishing.

Will it be bumpy? said Carol.

No bumps, I replied, automatically.

There's cloud over there, she said, pointing to a small mushroom of cumulus above the western hills.

That would be ten miles up, or maybe twenty, I said. It's a strato-vario-cirrus. Practically at the edge of space: there won't be any bumps today.

If you're lying, she said, I'll never forgive you.

The forecast was settled for three days at least, and as far as flying went, it could hardly be better. But it was nearly noon already, with a hot sun, and the morning's calm air might not be so calm any more. I was taking a chance, but it seemed to me it was now or never.

There were no bumps. I detoured to avoid the worst places, and flew up the lake, and by some miracle it was velvet-smooth all the way. We stayed high over the Dingle gorge and landed on the airstrip at Cotter's and parked the plane close to the trees at the top. Carol climbed out and stretched her legs and looked around, while I unloaded the kit.

Cotter's is one of the best of the old deerhunting strips. It runs down one side of an oval terrace that once was a river flat, aeons ago, and slopes a little bit down-valley towards the lake. It lies close to the trees on dry, patchy ground, and the rest of the terrace is covered with yellow grass, with a green swale through the middle where water leaks from the toe of the hill. There are mountains all around, rising through evergreen forest to rock and permanent snow, and the river is out of sight and sound, hidden in a deep ravine. When there is no wind the silence is uncanny.

How was the flight?

Carol smiles, unsure. I was scared the whole way, she says. I'll never get used to it, waiting for something to happen. But it doesn't matter now. It's beautiful.

We tied the plane down and carried the gear over to the hut, and boiled the billy and made tea. There was no one else there: no one in the entire valley.

We went down the steep hill to the river, down an old deer trail through the head-high manuka, and the first two fish — both in the same pool — were easy. I had seen only one and was casting to it when the second came up like a missile and drove my big, bushy Killer a couple of feet into the air. But it was hooked alright and I played it in and let it go. The other one, still feeding, was a little bit smarter, but it obliged in the end and I beached it as well. They were both rainbows, about three pounds, and although they leapt and dived and shook their heads they were not fat fish. Food is not always plentiful in a flood-prone stream like the Dingle.

It was two years since I had been here, and the river had changed. Many of the old pools had been blown away, leaving only a continuous cascade of fast-flowing water, useless for holding trout. New pools will form in the end, but this can take years, or even decades, and human life is not long enough to encompass many of these cycles.

We went through the timber above Cotter's and out onto the long, stony flat. There were no recent bootprints in the river silt, which, given the number of helicopter guides who operate in the Dingle, truly was amazing. Perhaps a recent spate had wiped the beaches clean, but, whatever the reason, we rejoiced in our splendid isolation.

Thoreau once said that 'in wilderness is the preservation of the world' — or words to that effect. And by wilderness we can be sure he meant a portion of the planet uncongested by human beings. How hard it is to think like that now, with a global population of more than seven billion, and how hopeless to argue that we should stop building more roads, stop building dams and irrigation schemes and expanding our GDP so that we can lure yet more eager termites and 'entrepreneurs' to accelerate the same dumb process.

There were colonies of rabbits in the Dingle when I first came here more than forty years ago. They lived in the dry gullies and flood-prone flats and it was always easy to shoot a few for a feed. They're all gone now — wiped out by 1080 and RCD, and I suppose we ought to be grateful to the visionaries who poisoned and infected and destroyed them. Like the deer they were a menace to the economy, and, such is the logic of human affairs, extermination was only to be expected.

But there are still a few hares — awkward, angular creatures, but pure poetry in rapid motion. There were two of them now, loping easily through the tall tussock on a sloping bench above the river. They stopped and faced each other and stood on their hind legs like kangaroos, and began cuffing each other around the ears and shoulders with their intermeshed front paws. They

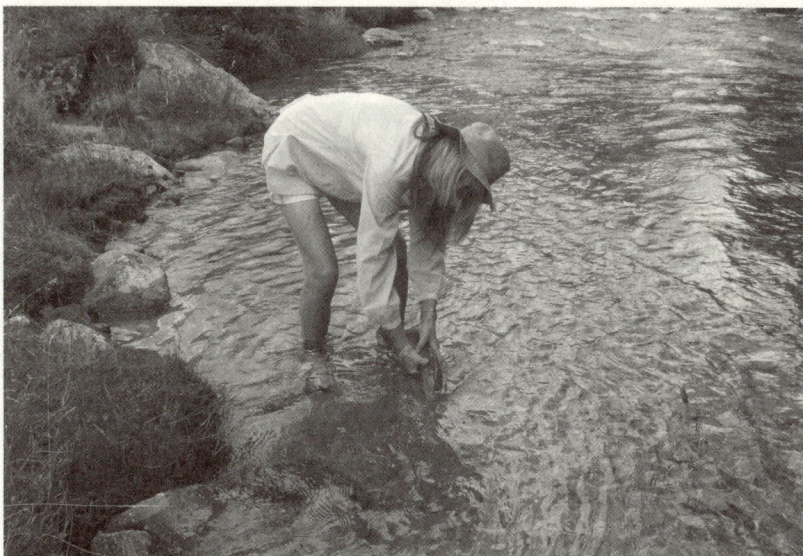

Carol releasing a rainbow.

were making love, not war, and when the preliminaries were over and the female amenable to her mate's attentions, she turned demurely and crouched in the grass and let him have his way. It didn't take long and he tried again, after another brief bout of boxing. But she bounced him off at the first prod and together they moved up the hillside. They paused on the ridge, side by side, and looked back down.

A side-creek came in, not far ahead, the debris of its outfall pushing onto the flat. We climbed over the boulders and were almost in the riverbed again when a big animal ran out of the scrub and stopped about fifty yards away. It had to be a deer, I thought, but it didn't look right, and it took me a moment to realise that it was something I had never seen before in such a place. It was a nanny tahr, shaggy-coated and solid-bodied, with legs much shorter than a deer's. It remained stock-still, quarter-on, watching us, and then ran full-tilt into the river and out across the open rocky ground and into the trees. Carol could hardly believe it.

Most of the riverbed had been rearranged by floods, and the upper flats, where the river once flowed in a channel cut deep into the grassy earth, have become a boulder-strewn graveyard that will not recover in our lifetimes. Fish may survive here and there in the fragmented water, but no one will ever again stalk those half-hidden defiles in the rich prairie grass, the tussock-heads almost touching above and the whole river a racing tunnel beneath, and see the great rainbows ten feet down in the clear blue icy water.

There are some good places left, and just downstream of Yard's Gully the best pool of all has survived through flood after flood for as long as I can remember. There were five or six fish, down on the bottom and swinging in the current, but the first one, when I hooked it on a loaded nymph, ran up and chased the others.

There were other changes to the valley. The family of magpies were gone from around Ben Avon hut — and the hut itself has been so perfectly restored that habitation is no longer permitted. It is a 'historic hut' now, a protected artefact, and you may look, but you must not stay. No more dream-filled nights in the old horse-blankets strung between rough frames of beech. No more camp-oven feasts in front of the big stone-flagged fireplace, with the flames roaring and the sharp smoke billowing into our eyes and the tears running down our faces. No more of such essential, enduring things that even the magpies, more likely than not, simply left in disgust.

I caught another trout in the gorge below Ben Avon, and then we went on back downstream — for once without a fish for dinner. In the lowland streams it makes no difference, but the days of harvest in the Dingleburn are finished for a very long time.

In the evening we sat outside the little two-bunk bivvy at Cotter's and watched the light slowly fade, and the mountains, across the gorge, retreat into inky blackness. There was no moon, and the sky was painted from horizon to horizon by the stars of the Milky Way — our galaxy — our little corner of the infinite.

A morepork called, and another responded, and we both joined in and were answered indiscriminately. The dry wood was chopped and the fire set, and we had an hour of grace while the last warmth escaped from the surface of the earth and the little owls moved closer. I'd love to see one, Carol said, but they stayed in the darkness of the beech trees. The stars burned in the cold luminous sky, and I lit the fire and we moved inside and cooked and drank wine till midnight.

Morning. The terrace was white with frost and awash in early sunlight, but the hut, tucked hard against the hill, remained in frozen shadow. I got up reluctantly and rekindled the fire and boiled the billy. Breakfast was brief. It was dead calm outside, and not a cloud in the sky, and the sooner we got going the better.

We hit one or two bumps, but not big ones. Carol gripped the steel cross-tubing that braced the wings, her eyes shut tight. Then the air was silky again and she began to relax, and we got home, safe and sound.

Huhus and beetles: a summer trout from the Hunter.

The Wheao before they destroyed it.

Rainbow fishing in the North Island.

Carol in the bush at Big Bay.

Bubble plays a rainbow.

Cloud clearing over West Otago.

Dave by the Cascade River, West Coast.

Pyke Valley, South Westland.

Dougal nets a brownie.

The Avid could go almost anywhere.

A sitter.

Jesz and Pete.

Crayfish from the Coast.

Two-Pies. Back-country bliss.

NINETEEN

The
Right
Man

The phone rang and it was my old mate Pete Adams, calling from Plymouth, England. We hadn't been in touch for more than thirty years, so this was a bit unexpected. Found me on the computer, he said. Find anything on the computer.

Pete had retired from his engineering business. He had made enough money, he said, and now was the time to spend it. He had located a few other old friends from university days in Belfast, and I was somewhat surprised to learn that most of them had also done rather well. You'd have had to be an idiot not to, Dave, he said. Given the times we lived in.

I thought it better not to dwell on this, and quizzed Pete about the whereabouts of various other contemporaries long lost sight of. They were all over the world, he said, and hardly any had remained in Ireland, and at least one of them — Jesz Fleming — was practically my next-door neighbour. We should get together one of these days, said Pete. After all, they were still making Guinness.

Next door, it turned out, was Western Australia. So I phoned

Jesz and had a yarn, and happened to mention that I spent a fair amount of my time fishing for trout. He seemed interested, so I described the glories of the Mataura, embellishing them not a little. Sounds great, he said. And in fact it's something I've always wanted to do. But isn't it incredibly hard to learn — casting and fly selection and all that? It must take years and years.

Nonsense, I assured him. Couldn't be easier. The stuff about it being difficult is all hot air put out by the poncy types who just want to make themselves look good and cut down the competition. Trout might be very beautiful fish, but they have tiny brains, so how could they be hard to catch? There's nothing to it, I said, and you could pick it up in no time at all.

A week or so later I got an email from Jesz. He had been talking to Pete, and had relayed my angling information. Pete was dead keen, he said. Pete, it appeared, had always fancied himself with a fly-rod, and while neither he nor Jesz had ever handled one, they were, on the basis of my encouraging testimony, busting to give it a go. Would it be alright, then, if they shot over to New Zealand in about two months' time, around the end of February? They were looking forward to mastering the piscatorial art and catching lots of fish.

I was caught. I was sunk beyond retrieval. I could hardly say no, please stay away — everything I told you was lies. These New Zealand fish are clever as hell. They're cunning as crocodiles, and nobody can learn to cast convincingly in anything less than a season. You have virtually no show of landing a trout. You'll be lucky even to see a trout. Even the experts get skunked.

I stayed at home for the next few days, trying to cook up some kind of half-plausible excuse to avoid the inevitable. Now and again, I reminded myself, the Mataura trout are easy. But they're never easy when you want them to be, and certainly not when you have a beginner hoping to snag one. Years ago, before I wised up, I'd taken a few hopefuls fishing. None of them ever caught anything, not even a six-incher — and that included the ones who already knew the basics of casting. Pete and Jesz were stuffed. I'd have to tell them the truth.

Jesz in the back country.

The next day, however, Peter Sutton came up from Invercargill, and, after I'd confessed my self-inflicted dilemma, he told me to relax. Don't fret, he said. Say nothing. Let the boys come out. Lay in plenty of grog, and get them to hire a guide.

But they're total greenhorns, I said. They've never fished for trout before, so how is that going to help?

Leave that to the guide, said Peter. It's his problem. And if they don't catch anything it's still his problem. You're in the clear. Just blame the guide.

There was logic in this — a fine, cynical, straightforward logic that I knew I couldn't improve on. We went for a fish that afternoon, caught nothing, and when Peter left he promised to make some inquiries and put me on to a guide. Trust me, he said. The right man is out there somewhere.

Peter was as good as his word, and he phoned me shortly afterwards. The right man, he said, is called David Murray-Orr, from Wyndham. He's an ace on the Lower Mataura, and from what I hear he could teach a wombat to dance the polka. Only problem, said Peter, is that he's tied up until a few days after the punters get here.

The boys arrived on schedule, all kitted out in unsuitable gear and fair jumping to get at the trout. I drove them down to Balfour, explaining en route that no fishing was planned for the next three days, on account of the lunar cycle. The astrological situation is very important, I said, because trout do virtually nothing without reference to the moon. But don't worry, I added, because in the meantime we'll practise casting.

Balfour Headquarters, well packed with hand-picked drunks, was humming nicely by the time we got there, and I was delighted by the effortless ease with which Pete and Jesz adapted to our local conditions. They recognised, almost intuitively, that the ancient traditions of fly-fishing involve much more than the mere riverside mechanics of trying to catch a fish. They identified, as though by instinct, with those relaxing and companionable rituals whereby generations of happy anglers have whiled away the passing hours and days when the trout are on the bottom. So completely, in fact, did they acclimatise, that we forgot to do any casting.

Day three was Guide Day, starting at six a.m. I cooked breakfast, a major effort, and got the boys into a car. I gave them written directions for the rendezvous, somewhere south of Gore. Then I went back to bed.

The rest of the crowd got up about noon, and there was another round of breakfast. It was a lousy day, overcast and drizzling. Some fanatics maintain that these are the best conditions for mayflies, but the big hatches were pretty well over, and the general consensus was that this was a day for tying flies, reading, and converting firewood into atmospheric pollution. The unspoken question, needless to say, was the situation on the Lower Mataura.

It was very late, well after dark, when the door banged open and Jesz stomped in, followed directly by Pete. His face was contorted, his hair was dripping, and he pointed straight at me. You bastard, he roared. You awful, conniving bastard.

I attempted to speak, but he cut me short. Not a fish. Not a goddam fish! We got soaked to the skin, and Pete fell in and was nearly drowned. And that bloody guide, the useless crook, he charged us twice the amount he said. And he hid in his car half the bloody day, and, and . . . Jesz ranted on and on.

I couldn't believe it. This was worse than my wildest and most desperate imaginings. I wanted to die, to disappear, to be anywhere else but here. I stood by the table, poleaxed, while Jesz raved on, flailing his arms and practically frothing with invective. Thousands of dollars wasted, and a lifetime's friendship all over. But then I remembered something — something about Jesz. Jesz had always been a joker.

I looked over at Pete, caught the gleam in his eye, the upcurve

Nothing could be easier. Pete with a keeper at Cattle Flat.

of his lip, and knew I had been completely suckered. Then they were laughing like pirates.

The photographs told the story. Fish after fish: glossy, speckled and beautiful. They had gone to several locations and fished a variety of water. There were fish everywhere. Look at this, look at that! Look at the monster that Pete had played through half a mile of river. God, it had been amazing. They had learned prodigious amounts, volumes in a day: they could cast, they could fish, and that guide — that Murray-Orr bloke — well, he was a bloody genius.

It was a big night after that, one of the most memorable ever. But it had been a long shot, and a close shave — and it had all depended, as Peter Sutton had said, on the right man being out there somewhere.

TWENTY

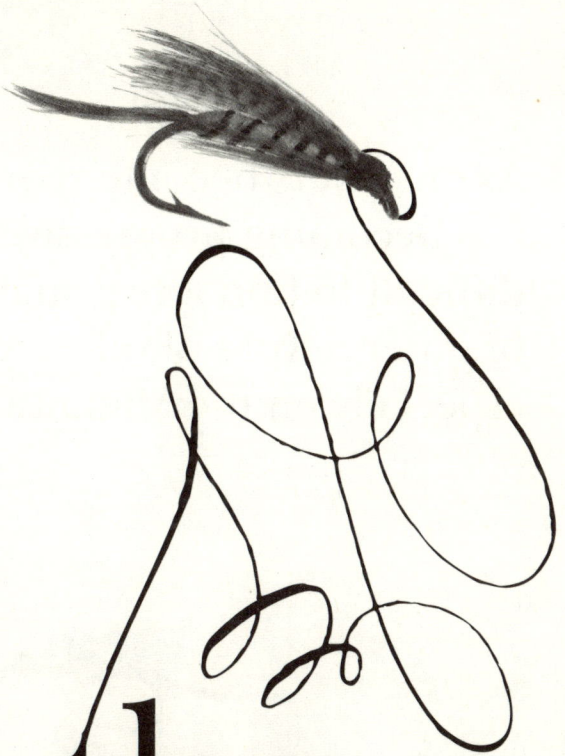

On the Beach

As our rivers become more crowded it is becoming progressively more difficult to find a reasonable piece of water devoid of other anglers, especially on the Mataura.

O ne solution to the problem, I concluded, would be to give up surface transport and commute to the fishing in the aeroplane. I could fly along the river, find an unoccupied stretch, and land on a paddock beside it. Not only would backtracking be eliminated but so would the dispiriting business of fishing for hours only to catch up on a gang of tourists who had already hoovered the water.

There is no shortage of flat paddocks along the Mataura — but even better, I realised, were the shingle beaches that are left exposed when the river is in normal flow. Every few hundred yards there is a fine big beach — a ready-made airstrip, exactly where you would want it.

I took off on a mid-April morning and cruised off down the river, keeping to the minimum height and banking alternately from bend to bend above the yellowing avenues of willows. The tourists had mostly departed and there was plenty of water to choose from, so I picked an angler-free stretch below the Pyramid Bridge, cut the power, dropped the flaps, and lined up on an inviting beach.

The wheels hit the shingle, rolled a few yards, dug in hard, and stopped. The tail came up and the nose went down and the prop smashed itself into fragments, sending a spray of stones and splintered wood into the air and across the water. It was an impressively short landing, no doubt about that. The plane was planted like a fencepost, tail high and fuselage vertical, and I was wedged just above the instrument panel with a close-up view of gravel. The angling was over for the day.

The season ended shortly after that and I had a think about the situation. I found a video about pilots in Alaska who regularly landed on riverbeds. What they used, and what I needed, it seemed, were purpose-built wheels — bush wheels — with big, fat tyres. These would marginally reduce the cruising speed, but spread the load when I hit the ground. They were guaranteed for sand and gravel, rocks, mud, and yard-high weeds. They could even put down on water, given sufficiently delicate judgment, although I thought that might be pushing things.

The wheels arrived six weeks later, airfreight from California. They were big alright, but they fitted easily on the undercart, and gave the RANS a potent, hunkered look, just like a genuine bush plane. I did a few landings on my local strip to get used to the different aspect, and then, shortly after opening day, I headed back down the Mataura.

The river was up. Not too bad, but just enough to cover a lot of the shingle. There were a couple of places that seemed alright from cruising height, but the amount of fresh driftwood when I got lower was enough to dissuade me from doing anything heroic. I dawdled home, flushing the ducks on the Waimea, and for the next month or more went fishing in the Toyota.

It was a wet spring, with several big floods, and by the time the high water and silt were gone I had driven to a dozen or more beaches and cleared away enough logs and stones to make them workable. I caught quite a few trout, but as often as not when I got to the river there were anglers already camped there — a useful reminder of why I had wanted to fly in the first place.

By the second weekend in November I was ready to try again. The river was back to its summer flow, with plenty of dry gravel. The mayflies were back too, and the trout were well fed and becoming harder to catch. They stayed under cover until well on in the day, so on my big morning I slept in and had a leisurely, late breakfast. Why disturb the tourists for no good purpose? I would show up for the one o'clock hatch, a civilised hour, and the nearest Aussie would be miles away. That was the plan, at any rate.

It was an ideal morning, a bright, blue day, a shoal of distant cirrus hovering over Blackmount, and I decided on an exploratory cruise down as far as Monaghan Road to check out the angler density. The river seemed ridiculously clear from up in the air, its long level pools unruffled by the slight breeze drifting upstream, and the darker stones of the riverbed were like fat fish in the deeper water. There were one or two vehicles under the trees, and several brace of anglers busily at work, close to the popular access points. But there were no bent rods, and no rises in the tailslicks — the little ones hadn't started yet — so I peeled away from the main river by the junction of the Otamita and skimmed across to Mandeville for a cup of coffee at the airfield.

It was eleven-thirty, too early for lunch, but the café was open and I found a seat outside under a tree. The air was warm and perfectly calm — the first settled weather of the summer — and down at the end of the runway a yellow Tiger Moth was just about to take off, but otherwise I had the place to myself. This,

Balfour International.

I decided, is not too bad. This is fishing as it was meant to be. Sitting at my ease, enjoying expensive legal drugs, savouring the promise of the day.

I listened to the drone of the Tiger. It levelled off at a couple of thousand feet, and dropped into a loop, and I thought of the river, just beyond the trees, journeying to the sea in its own sweet time, and the trout growing restless and the little nymphs shifting beneath their stones, ready for their great adventure. Yes indeed. No more dawn starts for me.

The best chance today, I figured, was about six miles back upstream, at a part of the river hard to reach from the nearest road. There were banks of willows and deep, shady water, cool on the hottest of days. The ripples were knee-high, cobble-bottomed, and full of nice two-pounders. There were bigger fish too, five-pounders, maybe, and there were no anglers when I flew down. I finished my coffee: it was twenty to one — close to zero hour in the mayfly universe.

Flying a light plane is wonderful fun, and just about as addictive as fishing. The best part, though — or the most exciting part, anyway — is bringing the thing back to earth again. This is the unavoidable moment of truth, when buoyant air meets terra firma, and only you can manage the transition. There's no way out of it, and it happens so very quickly. One moment you have an aeroplane: taut and intact, a responsive, beautiful, mechanical bird; and the next, if you don't get it right, a pile of wreckage.

There was a broad, curving beach halfway up my chosen bit of river. I checked the wind, which was zero, and came over the last paddock in a straight, shallow glide, with the nose well up and just enough power to keep the machine in the air. There was nothing to it at all. The wheels kissed imperceptibly and stayed down, and we rolled to a halt without even a touch of the brakes.

I got out of the plane and walked back along the beach. The big tyres had made no visible imprint, and the only mark on the shingle was the single track of the tail wheel — exactly what the Alaskans had specified. There were logs, half-buried in the shingle, unseen from the air, and I hadn't even felt them. I turned back at the end of the beach and went along the edge of the water. On the far side of the river, fifty yards away, ran a curving line of willow trees, overhanging a ripple that fell away into a long, slick glide, and in the middle of this, thigh-deep, half-camouflaged against the uprights of the trees, stood an angler.

He was watching me. He retrieved his line and waded ashore, and I went over to meet him. He was an American, Curt Nelson, from Connecticut. We shook hands and I apologised for my rude arrival. I'll go on upstream, I told him. My balls-up entirely. I must have been blind not to see you. But Curt would have none of that. Be my guest, he said, there's plenty of water.

We talked about the fishing, one eye on the river, and Curt had a look at the plane. He was an old bloke, about my age, and he and his angling buddy had been coming to New Zealand every southern summer for thirty years. The Mataura was their favourite river, the finest they had ever known, and the only season he had missed had not been by choice. His friend had died two years ago — died while fishing not far upstream from where we were now — and for a long time the magic had gone out of rivers and fishing. But now he was back, and the Mataura was as lovely as it had always been. And he would keep coming back, he told me, for as long as he was able to fish.

Mayflies were fluttering into the air, and five or six fish were rising in the shallow water at the edge of the beach, but Curt said they were sprats. The better ones were further out, and there was a four-pounder near the willows that he had raised and missed twice already. It's still going, he said, and I reckon I'm going to catch it.

I walked up to the head of the pebbly beach, and round a bend where the river surged through a deep narrow gut, and crossed over at the tail of the next pool. There were trout rising out in the middle, sipping at a froth of emerging duns — easy ones, I thought, and then I spooked them one after the other.

It didn't matter. There were plenty more, and I crept up to the next ripple and found a whole pod, ten or fifteen, close together, darting side to side down near the stony bottom. Now and again one of them would rocket up in a splashy rise, so I replaced the beadhead nymph with a Cul de Canard and dropped it in front of the nearest. It was a two-pounder, just what I wanted, and I got it in and banged it on the head and went back down and across the river to the plane.

Curt was still where I had left him, thigh-deep in the amber glide opposite the high hedge of willows. His cane rod flickered in the chequered light, moving the line in a lazy arc in the direction of his four-pounder.

I climbed into the plane and took off and went home. Everything had been perfect.

TWENTY-ONE

The
Truth

The problem with writing about angling lies in the fact that anglers have seldom been satisfied with the bare bones of what actually happens. Anglers, romantics at heart, want more than that.

Anglers appreciate, as far as fishing is concerned, that the truth is always negotiable. It mutates and shifts, bouncing in the synaptic labyrinth of the brain's unruly domain. The truth alters, sometimes subtly, sometimes dramatically, as elusive and mercurial as the trout themselves, as ungraspable as water.

Reminiscence is the final product, the ripened harvest of every angling adventure, and mere reportage betrays a failure to grasp this superior reality. The elements are not isolated: they live and breathe and interact — the river and its magical fish, the rain, the sun, the passage of years, the conversation of friends. Time passes, and these myriad components combine and transform into new and unsuspected compounds, so that in the end the truth becomes a distillate of everything that happened or might have happened.

Most anglers understand this. Embellishment is the essence of all fishing lore: the dark clouds thin and vanish, the sun beams down, the wind abates, and the trout conform, in retrospect, to the demands of our imaginations.

Most anglers understand this, but not all of them. There are no barriers to going fishing, and so, inevitably, there persists a sad minority who, in a well-ordered universe, ought to be playing golf. Never, in this world's travail, will these people escape the self-imposed bonds that frustrate them. Debarred by their own natures, they wade through false angling postures, adding days of woe to years of woe, lamenting their misadventures and spreading blight where joy should be ascendant.

These unfortunates, who are beyond all help, share one common defect. They cling as drowning men to what they think are the facts, and they believe these facts are immutable. They are literal people, objective people, and the imagination that alone might save them — that can transfigure all experience, even the worst, into something rich and strange — is beyond their natural capacities. The contamination of such afflicted must be avoided like the plague.

Hemingway thought we should lie outright, if necessary. Fishless days, Ernest maintained, were best restored by angling nights of limit bags and whisky. Some may demur. The less resolute will maintain that a core of truth is essential, even in the most trying of circumstances, even in the wake of disaster — that to simply invent the whole works may undermine an honoured equilibrium vital to the community of anglers.

There's not much risk. Complete invention is seldom required, if only because even the most cack-handed angler occasionally catches a fish. And let us not forget those glittering days when the river winks and the trout oblige and the duffer outfishes the expert. Such days are the pure gold of legend, perfect in every moment; why bother with embroidery?

Angling exists in a world apart — a world of illusions, makeshifts, sweet inventions. And the rules of this world, while it yet exists, are ours to interpret as we please. Here at least we roam at liberty: we are anglers, not actuaries.

The bite of a hook is tiny: its grip in the flesh of the trout no deeper than a pinprick — and its lodgement dependent on a measured strike that may be critical to half a second. The trout exists in a half-glimpsed realm, cold-blooded, distant in time as a dinosaur, and the angler deals in mystery.

The long cast lights on the water. The tiny fly floats, drag-free, on a perfect line to the waiting fish, which quickens, pivots, breaks the silken sheen of the surface. Time ceases. The angler's existence, up to now, is negated. There is only the breaking moment, the beating heart, the alien creature poised between life and extinction.

The rod tilts upward, decisive. The hook catches, scratching the jaw's hard flesh, and pulls free into the water.

The trout slides away, only slightly alarmed, its dark form swiftly dissolving. It was the only fish of that summer day. How big was it, and how beautiful?

Not a trace remains. The river glides on, its surface healed, and nothing observable has altered. Is there any difference, then, in the electric flux that comprises everything, between what happened and what nearly happened? What may authentically be made of a fragment of time now resolving into memory?

In the gathering dusk, in the hay-scented air, the angler walks in a kind of bewitchment. In his mind's eye he can see the fish, the shifting shadow, the emerald light, the image of curved jaws closing. In the muscles of his wrist he can feel the strike, and the hook hit home, and the surface of the river shatter. He can sense the terror of the living thing in its long run down the green wall of willows, and the strain telling, and the fish slowing, and the gift of control at last.

He is driving. The sun is setting. In the cavern of his mind, unbidden, a new narrative is forming.

TWENTY-TWO

Two-Pies to the Rescue

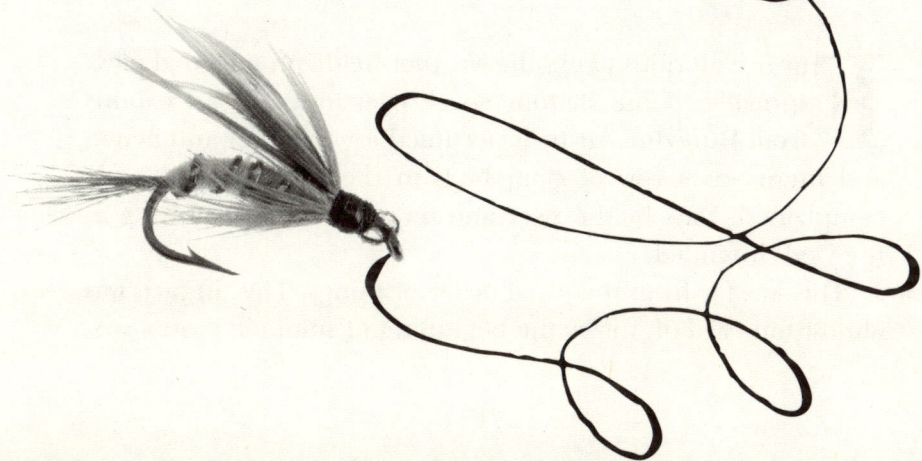

It was the end of the twentieth century, and the early season was a wipeout. There were lurid skies and sudden storms, then rain that melted the snow. High water and no flies — omens all, the sages confidently predicted. But the best of seasons start erratically, and by the end of November the rivers were in bloom again, with a bounty of trout the like of which had not been seen for decades.

F or five glorious weeks the weather held and the good news spread and the Balfour shack overflowed in an exodus from Dunedin. Air beds occupied every corner and bench and there was a row of camp-beds in the woodshed. Nobody complained. Days by the river and fevered nights: fly-fishing as the Gods intended.

This was far from the usual order of things. This, in fact, was almost unheard of, for by the beginning of summer, most years, the trout are becoming difficult. The early hatches have been and gone, and the willow-grubs are still burrowed deep in the leafy architecture of their willow hosts, growing fat on chlorophyll. Fishing can be slow as the days stretch out, when the idyllic-seeming waters of the Southland streams are seldom punctuated by feeding trout, and the tourist-anglers — the experienced ones — don't show up until the end of January.

But this was the year — the millennial year — when everything was allowed to be different. Anglers are optimists, opportunists. They live for the day, and the disasters of October were soon forgotten in the time of plenty that followed. All the rivers, simultaneously, were in perfect order, and there were squadrons of big trout rising in clear pools all along the Mataura. From Garston to Gore the river teemed, and further downstream to the sea at Fortrose, for all any of us knew. And they were civilised trout, emerging without fail to a late-morning hatch, retreating at noon — just long enough for lunch and a snooze — with an encore in the late afternoon. It was a sybarite's dream. No early struggle from a comfortable bed, no untimely wrench from slumber. Light in the window, a slow-dawning awareness of life and limb, the aroma of re-entry, caffeine, protein, an hour's siesta, maybe, and then a five-minute drive to the river.

Christmas came: holiday-time. There were boats on the river: plastic kayaks, rubber dinghies, little kids splashing in sun-warmed shallows, tents and caravans and fathers tossing hardware at the tantalising trout, so visible and insolent. Drowsy noondays and mild, warm twilights of campfires and beer and the smell of broom, and time peeling back, back to childhood, to the remembrance of summers long gone.

Dougal showed up with Bob Wyatt, who had fished the world,

but was new to the Mataura. They found a half-acre pool on a bend, just above the huts at the Tomagalak confluence, and one afternoon when the hatch came on the fish were too numerous to count. The flies hung in the air like a snowstorm, and Bob caught nineteen fish, including two six-pounders. It was maybe his best day ever.

Nothing lasts, and the good times, as they had to, came to an end, swept away in the sudden violence of a storm from the ice of Antarctica. The Balfour premises emptied out, while the local motels filled up with disconsolate, grumbling Australians. There was nothing to do but drink.

The weather turned feral. Flood and drought were simultaneous in watersheds mere miles apart. Gales alternated with breathless days, and frost with blistering heat. And as January gave way to February it was only at the rarest of interludes that fishing was more than an ordeal.

I went out every now and again, and fluked enough fish to at least keep trout on the menu. Then Kevin arrived, accompanied by Two-Pies and Turner. It was willow-grub time, by the calendar, but no trout appeared, not anywhere — and no willow-grubs were manifest either. Most days it was far too cold. The bigger rivers were in flood again, and the smaller ones, whose catchments had temporarily escaped, were crammed with despairing tourists. The tiny Waimea, just down the road, was a desolate termitary of Aussies and guides, bent double in the downstream blast or hunched up, foetal, under the banks.

We hung around for a week longer, cooking up stupendous feasts and lowering Kevin's stock of wine. But the weather just grew more vindictive until, mutinously bored, we got up early one day and set off for a drive round the furthest marches of Southland. There was a fine gale howling that morning, debris in the air, and felled conifers across the dirt road to Dipton. We retreated and detoured and motored on, past the Oreti and the Aparima and into the foothills and through Scott's Gap to the Waiau, stopping on the bridges, watching in awe the desperate antics of the Australians.

At Clifden in the late afternoon there were white-capped waves on the water. The wind blew down the great valley, shaking the girders of the old bridge, rocking the car and turning us back again, northward, in search of shelter. Dust billowed from the gravel roads, captured by the wind and flung over the fields, and sometimes, when a twist in the way turned far enough, we were enveloped in our own gritty wake. There was no escape, not even in the deep forest at the Borland, the big timber swaying, the river roaring.

Two-Pies said he had had enough, and we got back in the car, homeward bound, motoring through lanes of writhing flax in the eddying lee of Blackmount. The gale never eased. Dark clouds swirled around the Fiordland peaks, and the wild land, racked by the fierce, warm wind, seemed magnificently gothic.

At the Key there was an argument. Two-Pies was determined to go straight home. He had been driving all day, more than eight hours, and he alone in the car was sober. It's alright for you bastards, he moaned. Sitting in the back and snorkelling the grog and handing out the instructions. Two-Pies had a point, but Turner thought since we had come this far we ought to go left just a mile or so and have a look at the Mararoa. Kevin and I backed Turner.

There was a rental car in the park beside the bridge, squashed flat and almost hidden beneath a splintered macrocarpa. Australians, more than likely, said Turner. We got out and examined the wreck and lurched across to the bridge, leaning into the skittering wind, holding on to the railings. Two anglers were stuck in the middle of the river, perched in a half-sunk willow that had snagged in the swift-moving water. They were just audible and barely coherent. Their guide had been swept away, it seemed. A mate from Sydney. Top angler, fine fellow, now gone.

It was a tricky situation. The Aussies were making a fuss, hollering and gesticulating — but then, as Kevin pointed out, there was nothing new about that. Turner was dubious also. This is a police business, he said. There'll be official inquiries, and awkward questions. Missing guides, autopsies — it's not our

For five glorious weeks the weather held. Jesz being played by a rainbow.

scene. Take my word: there's always trouble when you get mixed up with Australians. And we don't have any rope anyway.

The last point seemed to be a clincher, but Two-Pies had decided to be difficult. Two-Pies is a Doctor of Philosophy, and nothing is ever straightforward. Not so fast, he said, squinting at the gibbering figures in the river. There are big issues to be considered here, moral issues, matters of life and death. Sure, they happen to be Australians, but never mind that, forget about that — in the final analysis these are people just like us. They're humans — they're fellow human beings.

This, I thought, might be pushing it a bit, but I try to stay out of anything to do with philosophy. I leaned over the bridge and had a good long look at the Australians. Still squawking, they seemed well wedged in the willows. The river was stable, neither rising nor falling, and it wasn't that cold, and there were bound to be more Aussies along this way soon, looking for fishable water. I scuttled back across the road, bent low, and opened the boot of the car. It was full of wine, so I opened a case and pulled out two bottles of shiraz — Australian shiraz, Rockford; Kevin's favourite.

Two-Pies charged up as I slammed the boot, arms waving above his head, protesting my apparent defection. He spotted the wine. He stopped, hesitated, grabbed the bottles and raced back over to the bridge. The Aussies fell silent as he leaned out from the parapet, a bottle raised, gauging the distance. His first throw fell short, but the second was right on target. The top was off in half a second.

It was dusk when we got back to Balfour. Dougal had arrived and was peeling a bucketful of spuds, and there were four mallard roasting in the oven. All we had to do was crack a fresh bottle and put a match to the dry pine already stacked in the fireplace. The events of the day, fresh in our minds, were elaborated for Dougal's benefit, and the talk then wandered far and wide — to politics, Australians, war, booze, and the impending end of possibly everything — and eventually to reminiscence of the recent past, the departed twentieth century. It was our century, after all: the best of times, the worst of times. But life was still tolerable, we had to agree. We were in fine fettle, we concurred, despite everything, relaxed in our semi-intoxicated ease, with the best months of the season ahead of us. Everything was provisional: the fishing, the weather, our tenure of existence. Good times would surely return.

Two-Pies was odd man out. He said hardly a word for a long time, lurking in a corner beside the door, draining his glass and refilling it. He had a bit of catching up to do, and was taking his handicap seriously. He went out for more wood, lugging in armfuls and piling it up, and responding only in monosyllables. We left him be, and were debating the innumerable ways to roast a duck when he pushed through the semicircle of chairs and lobbed his inevitable depth charge. Some people, he said — some people would just walk away from that kind of situation.

No one responded, and there was a long, loaded moment before he went on, addressing himself directly to Kevin.

You might not believe this, but they'd just walk away. Most of them would. They wouldn't want to be involved.

Really, said Kevin amiably. You don't say. The rotters.

No, Kevin. No, I mean it. Be a smart-arse if you like. But you'd have to agree at least that we didn't do that. It would have been easy, but we didn't. We faced the situation. We took all the circumstances into account, and — ethically speaking, I mean — ethically speaking we did the right thing.

Two-Pies was still in limbo, still wrestling with moral ambiguities. He stood in the hearth, agitated, looming over Kevin. What he needed was another half-bottle — but what he wanted was an absolution only Kevin could deliver.

Kevin sat back in his lazy chair, peering over his spectacles. His face, in the flicker of the flames, bore his trademark gangster grin, and his voice was furred with the wine.

No, Two-Pies, he said. You did the right thing — not us. You weighed all the circumstances and faced the situation, and there's no knowing what we would have done, left to ourselves. Probably something disgraceful.

Two-Pies stood motionless, waiting, and Kevin paused to take another swig from his glass.

I could say more, of course, but do I really need to? You are a shining example, Two-Pies. A beacon of hope in a darkening world. The calibre of your conscience humbles us. Your moral assurance and instinctive magnanimity. Your concern for the higher virtues. Your concern for those poor Australians. Your complete and total lack of concern for my two bottles of shiraz.

TWENTY-THREE

Two Australians

One day, just after Christmas, Two-Pies arrived back from the river with two Australians. It was about six o'clock on a beautiful evening, and we were sitting on the porch with tall glasses of gin, anticipating nothing unusual, so this was a bit of a shock. Not just one, but two Australians!

Australians, of course, are not necessarily unwelcome. There are no chauvinists in our brotherhood, and we have bona fide members from England, Iceland, Scotland, Tuvalu, and, dare I say it, Australia. There are no formal restrictions, but we do have to comply with official government policy, which, boiled down, means that Aussies have to be vetted.

Dyed-in-the-wool libertarians may protest about this. They may argue that all forms of discrimination are to be deplored, and to single out one nation among the hundreds in the world is indefensible. And there is some logic in this, but as loyal Kiwis we have little choice in a matter dictated not only by legislation but by centuries of popular tradition.

It is a reciprocal thing: Australians are wary of New Zealanders, and, quite properly, vice versa. It is a tradition with very deep roots, going back to the time when most Aussies were criminals and we were not. And it carries on to this day, even though our positions have become reversed, and New Zealand, in crooks per capita, is well ahead of Australia. History, in other words, has a lot of inertia, and we have to live with the consequences.

Yet here was Two-Pies, who is well aware of all this, strolling up the drive with two Australians that none of us knew, and obviously they were fishermen.

He had found them, he told us later, on a fast stretch of water above Monaghan Road. He was pissed off at first, because he had already walked about half a mile, and while he didn't want to go back he wasn't all that keen to fish along behind them. He thought about dodging up ahead for another half-mile, but he watched them instead, from the cover of some trees.

They were fishing a long, deep ripple. The water was fairly zipping along, and it was the sort of place where you need a bomb to get anywhere near the bottom. This works at times when there's a bit of colour, but when it is low and clear, as it was now, the Mataura trout are not too keen on bombs.

Two-Pies could hardly believe it. The two anglers were taking it in turn, working their way up the ripple and pulling out fish after fish. They got about twelve in the end, and put them all back, and they were heading up to the next bit when Two-Pies decided to investigate. These weren't average anglers. They were hotshots, total piscatorial wizards, and the thing to do, Two-Pies decided, was to intercept them and pick their brains. The thing to do, in fact, was to invite them home and interrogate them properly.

Two-Pies did the introductions and found some chairs, while Bob went inside and constructed a few more gins. The Aussies were from New South Wales, mates from way back — Peter Morse and Rodney Van Beek. They had been fishing in Southland for the past week, they said, and they had another week to go. It had been quite good so far, although they were disappointed by the absence of mayflies. We talked about the fishing — and not just

225

about trout. They were keen saltwater men, and had no end of tales about all kinds of fish. They might be Australians, but they seemed OK, and before they left we had arranged to meet again.

Dougal arrived early next morning, and we mentioned the two Australians. Dougal is at heart a trout fisherman, but for the last ten years he has become more and more interested in salt water. Peter Morse, he said. I know that name. He writes in the Aussie magazines. In fact I've got a book of his somewhere. He shuffled through the bookshelves, without success, but then he found a glossy sea-fishing magazine, and sure enough, there was a picture of Peter (alias Morsie) with a gigantic barramundi somewhere up in Queensland. He's a fly-casting champion as well, said Dougal.

Rodney and Morsie came round the next evening for a few more gins, and as well as angling we talked about casting. It was very complex and technical and didn't interest me half as much as the stories about fishing in Australia. I'm about average at throwing a line — or so I thought — and that's good enough for the kind of fishing we do in the rivers around here. But Two-Pies and Dougal were keen to learn more, so they set up a rod and handed it to Morsie.

Morsie made the line do things that I thought were contrary to the laws of physics. With no apparent effort he could send it to the end of the drive and right across the road and into an empty section on the other side. The line became a magical thing, defying gravity, levitating, doing anything that Morsie wanted, and I realised that I wasn't an average caster at all — I was a total plonker.

It was obvious what had to be done about this, and after dinner we made a date for Morsie and Rodney (who was also a demon with the fly-rod) to meet us on Saturday afternoon for a session of remedial casting.

The word got round, and by Saturday there was a party of nine on the Balfour rugby pitch, armed with rods and lines of various vintages and degrees of decrepitude. A majority of the hopefuls had some fishing experience, however minimal, but there were several complete novices — very keen, but didn't know fly-casting

Entente cordiale: Dave and Morsie at Nokomai.

from karate. This was going to be interesting.

It was a lousy day, grey and drizzling, but Morsie and Rodney were cheerful as ever. They had caught a few fish in the morning — on hatching mayflies, for a change — and after an introductory spiel on the theory and mechanics of the business they got stuck straight in.

Casting, for most fly-fishers, is something you pick up on the river. There are DVDs and books, of course, but it is only a tiny minority who ever take lessons. Fishing, after all, is a solitary, self-taught thing, and, unlike golf — where professional coaching has long been the rule — anglers still resolutely insist on doing it all on their own. I did, and so did all of my friends.

It was a big mistake.

We learned more in that couple of hours than we had learned in the past twenty years. The Aussies dissected our performances — identifying our individual faults and futilities, pulling apart the habits of a lifetime, and rebuilding them, step by step. The total beginners were most fortunate of all. With no bad habits to eliminate they went ahead with amazing speed, and by the end of the day they were more than good enough to get started on the river.

It was very merry at dinner that night: trans-Tasman relations had never before been so improved by random fortuitous circumstance. New bonds were formed, and ancient preconceptions simply disappeared, wafted away in a tide of bullshit, recollection, fabrication, and good Aussie plonk — and Two-Pies, three-quarters gone, proposed a toast to Australia. History is bunk, as Henry Ford used to say, and history was washed down the plughole.

We went fishing together after that, over the next few days, and caught some trout. Official policy notwithstanding, there are no chauvinists in Balfour.

TWENTY-FOUR

Sheepshit

The wind blew hard all night, roaring in the trees and rattling the tin on the old hut's roof. I wanted to go fishing in the morning, for despite the wind, there had been no rain, and all the rivers to the east of the Alps were low and clear.

Two-Pies had other ideas. No, he said. No fishing. We have to fix the bloody roof. Another gale like that and we'll be camping out in the open. Two-Pies was in one of his moods. There was no obvious sign of another gale. The budding day, in fact, was perfectly calm, and the warm sun was climbing a near-summery sky, and I could think of better things to do than sit on a rusty roof with Two-Pies, hammering in the leadheads. But, amenable as always, I did not pursue the argument.

By mid-afternoon the job was finished, but the best part of the day was gone and Two-Pies was still being difficult. We're low on food, he said. We are right out of eggs and bread and veggies. We're right out of meat as well. Did you know that? No meat!

Two-Pies replenished his mug of tea and chopped another six or seven thick rounds from a yard-long venison salami. He made

230

sandwiches of the salami between slabs of cheese and lined them up on the table. Man can't live without meat, he said. What we need to do is go over to Ray's place and borrow a rifle and shoot a hogget. Man needs a balanced diet.

None of this made any sense. Apart from the salami we had plenty of bacon and about a year's supply of canned stuff. But when Two-Pies is in a contrary state of mind it is best to be diplomatic.

Why don't we have trout for dinner? I said. We've put them all back so far, and if we don't knock off at least one we'll be just as bad as the tourists. And don't forget we've got tons of beer. There are heaps of calories in beer. And vitamins. It's a complete diet, beer, you know.

Logic is a powerful weapon. We finished the last of our lukewarm tea and collected our gear and headed out the door. We ought to try the gorge, said Two-Pies. Fegelmeyer says it's stuffed with fish. He was there about three weeks ago and he cleaned up. He got about ten in the ripples below the middle flat — and he let them all go — so we shouldn't have any problems.

Every angler has heard these stories, but now and again they turn out to be true, so I didn't make any comment. Fegelmeyer was probably bullshitting, but you never know, and we only wanted one fish anyway.

We walked down to the end of the paddock and untied the plane and pushed it away from the shelter of the beech trees. There was no damage from the wind, which was a bit of a miracle because there were branches down all over the place. We put the waders and boots in the luggage space and shoved the rods down the fuselage and checked the gas and got in and cranked up the motor. There was no wind to worry about, so when the motor was warm I just opened her up and took off across the river.

The gorge is about nine miles long. It has high, steep sides with native forest on top and so many bends you can never see very far ahead. The river tumbles down from pool to pool and there's no road, or even a proper track, but about halfway up, right beside the best of the fishing, there's a grassy flat that's just big enough to land on — and just far enough from the road-end to discourage most of the anglers.

We buzzed along, spying for deer on either side, and for trout in the water beneath us. There were a few rises, and one huge fish out in the middle of a big deep pool. The air was smooth — rare for the gorge, which usually funnels any available wind and ties it in knots and bounces the plane like a shuttlecock. But today it was dead calm, and we banked round the last bend before the flat in happy anticipation.

The flat was a carpet of sheep. There must have been about five hundred of the woolly bastards shoulder to shoulder from one end of the paddock to the other. There was hardly an inch of open ground, from the shingle at the water's edge to the timber upstream and downstream. There were sheep right into the water, standing in the river, up to their tits in it and swivelling their heads at us as we went over at about sixty feet. This wasn't part of the plan.

Shifting sheep with an aeroplane isn't all that difficult — one low zoom with the motor blatting and they'll be jumping around like fleas. But herding them is a different story. You have to keep them all in one mob, and all going in one direction. If you split them up you're stuffed, because they'll keep trying to join up — most probably just when you're landing. And biffing merinos with your undercart is a no-no with the cockies.

We were lucky. The job took less than five minutes. Half a dozen head-high passes and the sheep were all streaming into the jungle and heading off down the gorge. I did a last wheelie and skimmed in over the water and kissed the ground right at the edge of the shingle. The wheels locked when they reached the grass and we skidded along the flat in a fine, green spray of sheepshit. Very nice, said Two-Pies.

The river was a picture of perfection. There was a long, placid run at the edge of the flat, with a sandy beach on one side and a scattering of willows on the other. The water was autumn-golden and very clear, its surface flecked with yellowing leaves from the willows, and from where we stood we could see two fish lying

There was a little flat halfway up the gorge.

unperturbed on the riverbed in the deep water near the other bank. This will do me fine, I said. You can have the next bit.

Two-Pies took off with good grace. The plan was that he would kill a two-pounder for dinner and I would release any fish I caught. I waited till he was out of sight and then went further upstream towards the head of the pool; there was no point shagging around with fish that were sitting on the bottom. They were nice big fish, but they would be hard to get at, and they didn't seem to be feeding — and there were bound to be easier ones up in the faster water.

The first one I came to was where the ripple widened and deepened to blend into the throat of the pool. The current was slow and smooth — not yet a proper ripple — and I thought this fish would be choosy. But it wasn't. It nailed the nymph at first toss and barrelled off towards the willow roots that anchored the opposite bank. I leaned on it hard and turned it in time and coaxed it back up, and slid it onto a shelf of wet sand.

There must have been seven or eight fish in that ripple: lithe forms moving from side to side on the dark carpet of stones and sometimes flashing to the surface. I could have changed to a dry, but laziness prevailed, and I stuck to the lead-loaded Hare and Copper.

I caught five within forty minutes. They were taking everything that came along, sometimes spinning around and zipping downstream past me and then back to the same position. They all grabbed the nymph at the first shot, and they all reacted the same way — racing flat-out for the willows. It was just a matter of holding on tight and hoping the leader wouldn't break. Which it did, of course, on fish number six. But it was my own fault. I had landed five on the same fly, and the end of the nylon was chewed to a cobweb.

An image of that final fish is still clear in my memory. It was feeding in the shallow water at the very top of the ripple, and despite the confusion of the broken surface its outline looked impressive. When I set the hook it leapt, just once, and tumbled head over tail. Silver and black, it landed broadside and blew a horsetail of spray the whole way down to the willows. It was a magnificent brute of a fish, and I probably couldn't have stopped it anyway.

The sun had dropped to the rim of the gorge, and it was too late to go up to the next bit of likely water, so I went back to have a look at the two trout we had seen when we first arrived. They were still there, deep down, and I tried them with a bomb, but they just shifted sideways with each cast and then settled back on the riverbed. I wasn't going to catch them.

I walked over to the plane and stowed my gear, and was about to go looking for Two-Pies when I saw him near the top of the flat, wading across towards me. He was powering along, stumbling in the knee-deep glide at the tail of the pool, water flying everywhere. He came out above the big ripple and climbed up onto the grass, and I could hear him a hundred yards away, talking to himself, walking through the sheepshitty grass with his head down, muttering like he was certified. He hadn't caught anything — not a single fish. He couldn't bloody well believe it, he said. Not a single god-damned trout.

The light was just about gone, but the sheep were still skulking in the scrub and we got airborne without any bother. To the west, beyond a ragged black outline of mountaintops, the sky had turned red, and down in the murky depths of the gorge the river gleamed in silvery fragments.

Two-Pies had run out of invective. He peered into the gathering darkness, examining the higher gullies and slips, looking for deer, saying nothing.

The first bright stars had come out when we got to the hut, and circled round, and landed. We anchored the plane beside the trees and walked back across the paddock, and lit the lantern and put a match to the fire. Two-Pies was surprisingly mellow. He found a steak and kidney pie, encased in a tin, and once the fire was settled we baked it in the camp oven. We were hungry, and it was delicious, with a fat pastry crust and meat in a thick, juicy gravy. We had carrots and peas and parsnips as well, and lots of beer for the vitamins. The fishing business hadn't worked out, but, as Two-Pies remarked when we turned in for the night, at least we had got the roof fixed.

TWENTY-FIVE

Luck

There is skill, and then there is luck, and without a fair measure of both you're usually buggered. Not always, though. I can think of one outstanding exception: my old mate Bucky Buchanan. Bucky was a disaster, as careless and incompetent an angler as ever threw a line. But it didn't matter, because he was born lucky, and everything — money, women, ease of life — fell effortlessly into his hands.

We grew up together in Ireland, catching sticklebacks in jampots in the little streams, shooting rooks with airguns, and stealing apples in the autumn. Bucky's gift was already apparent.

There was a golf club at the edge of town, where the local lawyers and doctors and their wives played on fine weekends and evenings. They had put a dam on a stream to make a little lake and stocked it with rainbow trout, and by the time Bucky and I were nearing our teens the lake was three-quarters fringed with bulrushes and alive with lovely fish.

When school got out at three o'clock Bucky and I would go to the lake and hide our bikes and creep like Indians through the rushes. We had bamboo sticks and jampots of worms, and if none of the lawyers were around we would lob a cork float with a dangling worm out into the weedy water. Then, nestled in the thicket of rushes, we would watch the floats bobbing gently until, within minutes at the most, a trout would come along.

Float-fishing isn't all that different from the more poncy sorts of angling. The basic elements are exactly the same — a rod and a line and a lure — plus the float to make it more interesting. Who can forget those boyhood excitements: the first nod of the float, and then its twitchery to-and-fro when to strike will be premature? Steady. Steady. Stay calm. Watch and wait. Down goes the float — all under. Now! The braided line comes solid. No reel. No damping. Just the bamboo twisting like a living thing, and the fish leaping, out there at the edge of the reeds.

Now and again the golfers got bored and shut us down by dumping their clubs and doing a bit of fishing. They had a wooden jetty and a tipsy boat and they would row around for an hour or so and cast flies and occasionally they got a trout. They never used worms, which seemed dumb to us, watching from the bulrushes. But mostly they whacked balls round the golf course and left us undisturbed.

One fine day, with the sun out and dragonflies choppering this way and that on the glittery pond, Bucky took a chance. He left the shelter of the rushes and strolled round to the jetty and got into the boat and rowed himself across to a deep place we could never reach. I watched him, envious, as he shipped the oars and tossed his float into this new domain. The response was almost immediate: the float went down and the trout was hooked, and Bucky, exultant, grinned across at my lair.

The trout went under the boat and Bucky stood up to deal with it. He leaned too far and the boat rolled over and Bucky fell in with a great splash and went under the boat as well.

He came up again, coughing and spouting water. He couldn't swim, and neither could I, so things weren't looking too good for lucky Bucky.

But I needn't have worried. Three lawyers appeared like magic. They all dived in and swam out and grabbed Bucky and hauled him back to the shore. They turned him over a few times to let the water run out of him while more lawyers and doctors sprinted down from the clubhouse with a big tartan rug, followed by a posse of wives. This was more fun than golf, any day of the week. Hip flasks appeared and everybody had a few chugs — including Bucky. Then they hoisted him shoulder-high, wrapped in the rug, and the whole procession headed up to the clubhouse.

Bucky came home much later that night, drunk for the first time in his life. It was great, he said. They had stoked a big fire in the clubhouse and dried him out and one of the pretty wives had kept dosing him with hot whiskies. When they asked him what had happened he said he had borrowed the boat for a little paddle and the damned thing had tipped over. The day was so hot, explained Bucky, and the boat was just so tempting. He never said anything about fishing and nobody was any the wiser.

Bucky was made. He got invited back to the golf club any time he wanted. They gave him beer and whisky. They were so pleased with rescuing Bucky they more or less adopted him. They turned him into a kind of mascot — plucky little Bucky — and one day when Bucky casually mentioned the fish in the pond they bought him a rod — a real rod with a Mitchell reel — and took him out in the boat and taught him how to cast with brand-new lures and play the trout and land them with a net. That's when I knew for sure that Bucky's luck was something out of the ordinary.

The years passed and we finished school and went off into a world that in those days was still only half-explored, mysterious, and full of possibility. I lost sight of Bucky for several years, until a letter arrived, with a postage stamp from Canada. Bucky was running a goldmine in British Columbia, up in the mountains at a place called Antler Creek. It was great, he said. There was swags of gold, but, even better, there were rivers teeming with all kinds of fish, and forests full of animals. He needed help with the goldmine, he said, and I was just the man. If I was agreeable he would send the ticket.

He met me in Vancouver and we drove downtown to the Army and Navy store to buy the gear we'd need for the adventures that lay ahead. We filled the truck. We walked on a beach by the Pacific Ocean, thinking of salmon and sailing ships — and Bucky took me to Stanley Park to see the totem poles and the polar bears and flamingos. Everything was new and brilliant.

On the road north Bucky explained the situation. The goldmine was not exactly his, he said. But it was just as good. It belonged to Julie — a friend of his — a Canadian girl whose father had given it to her to keep her out of trouble. There was a manager, and some miners, producing the gold. Julie was in Kathmandu, and there was nothing much for Bucky to do until she decided to turn up again. Which could be a while, said Bucky.

We never went near the goldmine. We went to the Okanagan and fished for rainbows in clearwater lakes surrounded by mighty forests. The wildlife, compared with Ireland, took a bit of getting used to. There were animals bigger than people. There were bears and moose and several kinds of deer. There were cougars and wolves, and total oddities like skunks and porcupines, and wherever we went there were tiny chipmunks, raising families in the back of the truck and stealing the bread and biscuits. Raccoons, too — until finally we learned to string the stash from a wire between two trees. Eagles watched us through the day, and hissed at us from the treetops, and there were ospreys on nearly every lagoon, crashing in spray and staggering up, laden and barely flying. We shot fat little grouse with the .22 and fried them side by side with the red-fleshed trout, and at night, as we drank Gallo by the heaped-up embers, the cry of the loons in the velvety dark confirmed our endless good fortune.

One day, deep in the bush by an unknown river, a canoe appeared and slid up to the shore, and two men got out. They were Englishmen — or they had been, long ago. They had come to British Columbia for a holiday, in 1929, and had never wanted to go home. These men, it seemed to us, were more than just old — they were revenants. They seemed to go back to Lewis and Clark, to the voyageurs and the mountain men, to Daniel Boone and Davy Crockett. The river was the Nass, they told us, and it would take a week to get out, in the direction we were going. We gathered some driftwood and lit a fire and the old blokes brewed coffee and showed us the two trout they had killed — bigger fish than anything we had seen — which they had caught on flies. Dry flies.

The end of summer caught us unawares. The leaves changed almost overnight, from green to gold, and then to a pulsing crimson that illuminated the mountainsides. Then winter came, and the land turned hostile. Rubber hardened and broke like glass, and tow bars snapped unexpectedly. We drank Canadian Club, and put antifreeze in the petrol. Bucky wanted a moose for meat, and we found a bull and a cow, standing side by side on a forest track. Bucky wound down the window of the truck and shot the cow — better eating, he said. Then we packed and fled south, back to Vancouver — Canada's San Francisco.

Bucky had another friend, a fey, superior creature who sang in a band and lived on West Third Avenue, in an old three-storey wooden house that shook all day to Jefferson Airplane, Janis Joplin, Country Joe, Jim Morrison and The Doors. We were given

Dave and Bucky with moose head in
Vanderhoof, BC, Canada.

beds at the top of the house, and the winter passed in a glorious chemical haze divorced from normal time.

In spring, not long after the ice had groaned and cracked and jostled down the rivers, a letter arrived from Asia. Things had changed in the wider world — Julie had found enlightenment. She was living on a mountain near Kathmandu, in an ashram full of fellow seekers and their spiritual leader, a skinny, mesmeric guru. She was happy, she said: she had glimpsed the truth, the secret of life. But the path was narrow and the road was hard. No sex, no drugs, and — as far as Bucky was concerned — no more cheques from the goldmine.

Bucky read the letter and handed it to me. He watched me read it and then he laughed, and I thought he had blown his fuses. Maybe he really had been in love, truly in love, and now he was lost. His luck had finally deserted him. But it was nothing like that, as I might have known. It was something else: something that hadn't been mentioned. His aunt had died a month before — his favourite auntie, Eileen — the one who had gone to South Africa when she was sweet sixteen and married a Boer with swags of loot. No need to panic, said Bucky.

It was hot that spring in the wilds of British Columbia, and each bright day was a revelation. We saw a bull moose in a swamp, trailing a dark wake in the weed-green water, his entire body invisible. We camped in a cloud of hummingbirds, scarlet and blue, no bigger than the dragonflies on our lazy pond in Ireland. We drove. We moved incessantly, along the foothills of the Rocky Mountains, from the Yukon to the American border, discovering at random the rivers and lakes and their bounty of fish, and Bucky's luck stayed with him, primitive and feckless as ever. Grayling, whitefish, kokanee, char — it seemed that he had

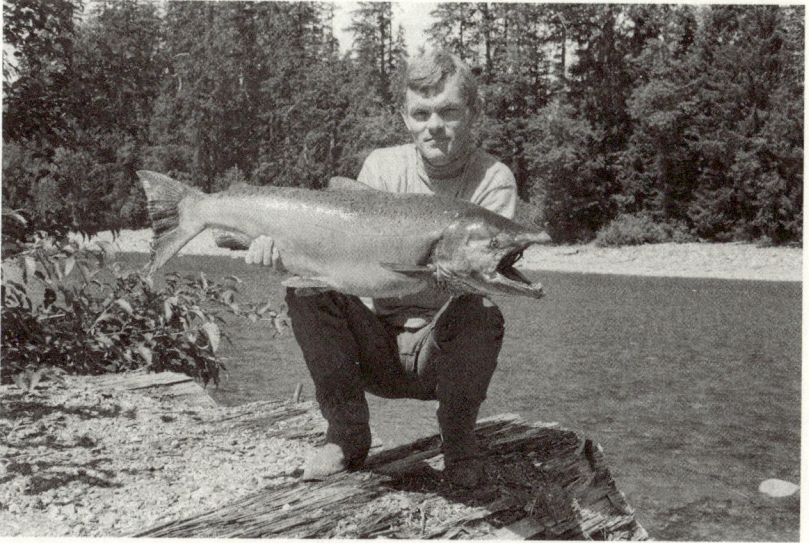
Dave with a king salmon by the Kitimat River,
BC, Canada, c.1970.

rights to all of them, despite any relevant expertise. He caught fish there was no point in catching, like the four-hundred-and-fifty-pound sturgeon in the Nechako that he snagged on a bucket-sized grapple and then had to park for a week, tied to a tree, while he found an Indian who knew what to do with it.

One day there was a story in the paper about a salmon that had been caught in the Skeena, down near the coast at Terrace. It weighed more than a hundred pounds — bigger than the schoolboy who landed it. There was a picture as well, and that was enough for Bucky. But the Skeena, when we got there, was a raging flood, grey and opaque as concrete. We hung around Terrace for a week, and then packed up and moved over to a smaller river in a separate catchment about thirty miles to the west. It was everything we had dreamt of — clear water flowing in rapids and pools through little glades in an unbroken forest of gigantic trees whose topmost branches were lost in the summer sky. The salmon were running and we could see them, swaying deep in the bellies of the pools, or rolling on the top, halfway out of the water. We fished with big spoons and heavy line, and caught twenty-pounders, and a few that were close to thirty. They were magnificent fish, ripping through the snag-cluttered pools, upstream and down, or sulking on the bottom, immovable. We caught several of them every day, and lost far more.

One morning, a bit earlier than usual, we left our camp on a dry river bench and went down the logging road to W4, our secret salmon-possy. There was a huge dead cedar across the river that we used as a bridge to a beach on the other side. The mist was thick that morning, settling in beads on our woollen shirts and hazing the shadows between the trees. Bucky was in front, and we were well out on the log before we saw the bears. There was a mama bear with two big cubs stopped one behind the other, about twenty feet ahead of Bucky. For a moment there was a stand-off. We stood still and so did the bears. Then mama bear moved forward, and I moved back, and so did Bucky. The log was slippery but I went fast and got to the bank and looked over my shoulder just as Bucky jumped into the river, followed by mama bear. I could see them both underwater, trailing bubbles, Bucky swimming the wrong way, out into the middle of the river.

The bear came up and looked around, but Bucky was still submerged. Then his head came out and mama saw him and was after him like an otter. She was moving a lot faster than Bucky, but Bucky was in the main current. I stood on the high bank shivering, remembering all the stories I had heard about mama bears with cubs.

The pool was about a hundred yards long, with a curve at the end that finished in a rapid. That was where the bear caught Bucky, in water about knee-deep. She grabbed him and pulled him to the shore, and then she let go of him, dropped him limp in the shallows. She prodded him and cuffed him with one paw and then stood still for a moment, looking at Bucky and then away, and back again at Bucky. Then she moved a few paces sideways and scooped a black, spent salmon from a channel among the stones. Bucky lay like a dead man.

We bought a bear rifle after that and went on fishing the Kitimat, and caught some big fish, but nothing close to a hundred pounds. My best was just under forty and for once it was better than Bucky's. Don't get excited, he said — the real ones don't come till the fall.

But by the fall it was all over. Julie came back without notice. She flew into Terrace one rainy afternoon when the last of the king salmon were dying and the first coho were leaping in the lower river. She hired a car and found where we were, camped on our old spot by the Kitimat. She had had enough of Kathmandu. There were bugs in the beds, and the food was crap — not a decent T-bone in the whole damned kingdom. It was amazing she had lasted so long, she said. The Americans had all come down with the shits, and the guru, of course, had turned out to be a lecher. Her enlightenment had worn off — or maybe it had taken a different turn, which now included Bucky. In any case our plans had been rearranged, because Julie was irresistible, even without the goldmine. She was half-crazy and capable of anything, and put together in a way that just about guaranteed trouble.

Life in the bush was over. We piled everything into the truck and drove non-stop all the way to Vancouver, where Julie, it turned out, had already arranged the wedding. Bucky went down to West Third for a stock of herbal necessities, and bought new jeans to get married in, and we drank Jack Daniel's until late every night with Julie's mother. Bucky seemed sideswiped most of the time, but happy, and when the best man bit was over I borrowed some money and got a ticket to Australia.

I bought a fifth-hand Holden in Sydney and drove west, across South Australia to the Nullarbor, where the money ran out at a place called Streaky Bay. I found a room above the pub, and after a week or so one of the local fishermen gave me a job, diving for abalone.

At Christmas I got a few letters from Ireland and a card from British Columbia. Things were going well, said Bucky. He had caught a few salmon in October, and shot a deer and a moose. He was busy at the moment, but would like to come and see me sometime — in a year or two maybe, when he got organised.

Not very likely, I figured — but again I was wrong. Four years later he arrived, and I picked him up from a dirt strip just outside town. He was tired from the trip, but he looked in good shape, and his eyes lit up when he got to the pub and heard about all the marvellous things we could do in Streaky Bay.

The sea was a world apart around Streaky Bay in those days. There were submarine jungles of amber kelp, and innumerable fish — and abalone to pay the bills. And since Bucky had never done any diving before, he was rapt. Then he discovered I had a hang-glider — an old Moyes single-surface kite that I used to fly off a headland down the road. It was pretty easy, I told him, so Bucky declared he would do hang-gliding. He studied the ads in the magazines, and sent away for the latest hot-dog machine — a Lancer, made in Auckland, New Zealand.

Days on the ocean, the world far away, cool evenings, wine and beer: there are worse places than South Australia. We explored the coast and searched the beaches, looking for ambergris, and made a few trips into the desert, and Bucky bought a special camera, mail-order from Adelaide, to take pictures when he was diving. He had to have pictures to take home, he said, or Julie wouldn't believe him.

He carried the camera with him everywhere we went. It was a bulky thing, and leaked all the time and got caught in the seaweed, and Bucky wouldn't stay close to the bottom when we were hunting for abalone. There wasn't enough light, he said, and the fish were just little buggers. He kept hanging around in the open water, where the big fish lived, and where he hoped to get a shot of something spectacular. I watched him one day, high above the canopy of the kelp, when hundreds of tuna suddenly materialised all around him. One moment there was nothing, and the next they were there, a wall of big silver tuna, their heads and tails overlapping, and all that was left of Bucky was a rope of bubbles shimmying up to the surface. And then in a flicker they were gone.

Bucky never worried about sharks. He said I was an ignorant Paddy, and produced a heap of statistics that I think he invented himself. You were more likely to be hit by a dead satellite than eaten by a white pointer, he said. The fishermen told him he was nuts, but he just bought more beer and told them to relax — the sharks were all in their heads.

We went diving or fishing most days, but Bucky wanted to start flying, so I gave him some lessons on the Moyes, running down hills and lifting off and skimming along near the ground. His landings were always crashes, but he was alright when he got up a bit — he could do turns, and climb and dive, and before long he was soaring the sea breeze above the cliffs, which could keep him aloft for hours.

The Lancer arrived. It was trickier to fly, but by that time Bucky was fully fledged. He seemed completely relaxed in the air. He could sense the wind, feel the slightest waft of lift, and anticipate its movement. He would catch little bubbles of thermal, spinning upwards in the tightest of turns, leaving me far behind. He didn't need luck — he was a natural, for the first time in his life.

On the fourteenth of February — St Valentine's Day — we took off about noon from the cliffs to the west of town, surfing the wave from the sea breeze, and pushing inland as far as the lift would take us. The air was cool near the ocean, but the ground was hot, and there were thermals bouncing everywhere. We would catch a bubble, circle around, and scoot up a few hundred feet till we lost the ride and had to find another one.

It was wonderful flying, and soon we were higher than we had ever been, far inland, going up in a great blanket of rising air, and accelerating where faster currents were punching through. Bucky could easily have left me, but he stayed close. He would circle around and dive at me, flashing past, zooming up and away. He was unconstrained, and the air had become warm away from the coast, and I was thinking it was time to be heading back when we went into a nuclear bubble heading for the stratosphere.

The Lancer was a more capable machine than the Moyes, and this was a mighty geyser. It was a vertical gale, straining the wire sinews of my kite, flexing the keel and spar. Bucky couldn't resist it. Soon he was just a small, distant patch, a black crucifix, circling and dwindling in the hazy blue as I wrestled with the wind, trying to get back to earth.

That was the end of Bucky. He was swallowed by the sky, and nothing was ever found of him. He must be still out there somewhere, in the desert, his bones white among the adders and the goannas, in whatever remains of his kite. Or maybe he came to the ground alive, too far to walk without water. It comes to the same thing anyway.

The sound of a river, running on stones, a limpid New Zealand sky. The Mataura sweeps in a broad arc through rough paddocks of ryegrass and clumps of thistles. The air is clean, with the warm scent of broom, and bright rags of cumulus sail above the willows, masking the light at intervals and blanching the river's skin. The morning's scant hatch of mayflies is over, and the trout are safe, for the moment. The Mataura is temporarily fishless.

Time is not the same on a river, as every angler eventually learns. It can speed up, or stretch out — and sometimes it can slow to a halt, and the laws of entropy are suspended. Rivers have strange capacities. They are the nearest to living things that the inanimate world has begotten. They live and die, through aeons; they move and change with the seasons, with the rainfall, with the passage of clouds in the blue. They have moods: now smiling, now malevolent. They are far from inscrutable, as some people have said — they are eloquent. They hiss in the sleet and purr in the noonday sun, and I am sure that the old North American Indians were right: when the last river dies, then so shall we.

A hare moves through the patchy grass towards me, loping in slow motion. It stops and sits upright and raises both front paws, as though in prayer. It tilts its head a little and swivels its long ears over its triangular face and massages its ears and face with both narrow paws, over and over, closing its eyes as it does so. It looks up, and suddenly perceives a human, mere yards away on the river bank. It hesitates, its brown eyes wide. Then it turns and sashays away through the grass, unhurried.

My mind goes back to the creatures I used to kill in Ireland. I remember the fields where we hunted, and the hawthorn hedges and the swift, tea-coloured rivers, and the first trout I ever caught in a river. And then the salmon — the rivers of British Columbia, the forest and the mist — and the powerful, incredible salmon. And, inevitably, I think of Bucky Buchanan.

Bucky was lucky. I used to have no doubts about that — until one February morning in the sky above Streaky Bay. Then whatever it was — his gift in life — was cancelled. The providence that had stood by him so long had deserted him, revoked his special entitlement. And the question returns to baffle me: how to interpret the ebb and flow of fate in the dumb lottery of our lives? What should we want, and what would we settle for, given the choice? A brief, golden time — or the standard ration of seventy years, of ups and downs, normality? Or, trapped in the timidity of our blood and flesh, would we prefer a full century of tedium?

The river moves past beneath my feet, and a small trout breaks the surface. Spinners are falling, wings glinting in the sun, and I lift my rod and slide down the bank into the water. The Mataura is becoming alive again, and my question will never be answered.

Acknowledgements

My thanks to Bob South, of *Fish & Game* magazine, who first published many of these stories in briefer form. And to my old friend, Barbara Larson, of Random House, for the impetus to write this book in the first place.

For more information about our titles go to
www.randomhouse.co.nz